CW01360035

PROFESSIONALIZING STRATEGIC SYSTEMS MANAGEMENT FOR BUSINESS AND ORGANIZATIONAL SUCCESS

Introducing the CCIM Three-Leg Stool

TERRENCE L. FARRIER, PhD

authorHOUSE®

AuthorHouse™
1663 Liberty Drive
Bloomington, IN 47403
www.authorhouse.com
Phone: 833-262-8899

Published by AuthorHouse 05/25/2021

ISBN: 978-1-6655-1537-5 (sc)
ISBN: 978-1-6655-1535-1 (hc)
ISBN: 978-1-6655-1536-8 (e)

Library of Congress Control Number: 2021904051

Print information available on the last page.

Interior Image Credit: Otis (Sonny) Olson

Illustrator: Ernest G. "Sonny" Olson (original artwork)
Editor: Dr. Anthony Lolas

This book is printed on acid-free paper.

Change is hard, especially if you are unsure where you are going. In a time of great societal stress, Farrier's out-of-the-box experiences in academia, military, corporate and business counseling bring fresh insights on how to deal with change. This is not your typical business textbook full of jargon and new theories. It is a practical application on how to analyze a changing business and/or societal environment and develop strategies for dealing with it through continuous improvement.

Benjamin M. Howe, APR
COL (ret) U.S. Army
Principal, Howe Communications

This book allows business and organizational management and employees to bind their concepts into practical and scalable applications that work! The "must do" is replaced with not only "why" but a concept of "how" while it fits those concepts into a program that is actionable for all. Without being too prescriptive, this book precludes failure by helping managers and decision-makers stay focused. Just like short versions of diets fail, so do mast management tools. Lessons learned from them last a little while and then everything goes back to habitual weight gain because the focus for improvement is lost. Any manager, whether civilian or government, who wants to improve their business or organization can apply the concepts of this writing to help them stay profitable and successful.

Contents

Foreword

She had fought a good fight, but she was dead. It was heartbreaking. There was nothing more to be done. Her ailments were just too advanced, and had become too complicated to develop good solutions to save her.

Her examiners, all from diverse fields, had tried everything. Now, her corpse lay before them. Astonished, they could not believe they couldn't find a remedy to side-step her demise.

Her spouse and her children would soon know they had lost a confidant and a provider. She was not human, but the loss and damage inflicted was just as real. She is your company, or your organization. Save her!

More than a few companies and corporations must fight to stay alive. As the needs to train and retain employees to keep up with ever advancing technologies increase, the processes to keep them functioning and profitable must change also. Change for change sake alone, can and have killed a few of them. Unfortunately, some of those efforts were just to hide the inabilities of some of the staffs who work within them. The result is still death.

Unless the stakeholders and staff can thoroughly research the pathway and obtain treatments for the company, it will slowly die. It took time to get to the state some companies and organizations are in. Some are already teetering on the brink of death, and yet some do not realize where the symptoms hide and are therefore dying slowly – but assuredly.

This book reveals a way to get past the snapshot remedies that many business examiners offer. It ties together those snapshot concepts that, at first glance, provide sustainable solutions. It is truly both a science and an art to conceive, adjudicate, and make actionable business operational solutions that last past the short term. The science combines the different management approaches to those short-term solutions, to provide an actionable and sustainable result. The art is communicating those solutions to those who are responsible to keep the science as pure as possible, and to provide the reasons that their responsibilities are imperative to long-term survival of their company or organization.

A multiplicative gap exists in both the academic and the practitioner's experiences congruent to the academic business capstone training and the communication and operating capacities provided within the corporate senior and middle-manager's tool kit. Once this information is digested, it should allow better outcomes for the schools and businesses they serve. Management in almost every field imaginable are complaining about the glut of information they receive that makes it difficult to make sound business decisions that can make a difference in the long-term. While some fractural information might be gained from each venue, those inputs are seldom focused to help inculcate the overall communicative and operational needs which are required to overcome the inclusive health of the company or organizations those managers serve. This book ties those concepts into a scalable and functional management system.

Universities struggle to prepare management capstone graduates for opportunities so that they might understand the diverse disciplines required of them to enter the workplace with the skills necessary to manage the businesses and organizational processes. Independent theoretical disciplines on their own are often achieved; however, the critical skills required of managers to step into inter-disciplined operations are most often not. Understanding where this gap exists is crucial for business schools, university leaders, and business practitioners whether they are locally or internationally focused. Providing experienced insights as to how business disciplines work in unity will improve the level of understanding and the profitability of businesses that utilize systems thinking.

Additionally, most companies are built to service a particular source of customers or clients. In efforts to serve various customer bases, some fluid and some static, independent departments or siloed divisions within companies can begin to vary outside the intent of the company structure. They begin to serve customers who don't strategically fit the mission of the corporation. While stretching to service more customers or clients is not all bad, the uninformed companies can find themselves wrestling with the ability to service and support them. It is wise for companies to plan reviews of their operations to make sure they are not servicing too wide a berth of customers at the cost of losing resources that might be better spent on legitimized and vetted core customers. These independent silos can quietly, slowly, and as assuredly rob businesses of those resources needed to develop and compete elsewhere by draining time, personnel, or funds.

The systems thinking approach, using the Change and Continuous Improvement Management (CCIM) 3-Leg Stool, will fetter out where these silos exist, whether they exist in human resources, operations, administrative processes, information systems, transportation, shipping, warehousing, or otherwise. Also, it can articulate the *why* and the realization that every managerial decision made needs to support the organizational whole to remain competitive. If you are a manager at any level and strategic competitiveness or if a systems approach to stay in business for the long run interests you, it is fortunate as you are reviewing a concepts tool to possibly achieve both - at this moment.

Also, if you are attempting to break the gridlock associated with the corporate management structure so that you can be the go-to individual associated with cross-division communication, you should read this book. It doesn't matter if your company utilizes agile, Kanban, just in time, or is set in civilian or military operations, the systems approach in this book can provide greater insights into the complexities of systems thinking and turn them into actionable processes.

Further, it will provide managers reasons why systems thinking is increasingly important to remain competitive and survive in strategic markets. It doesn't matter if you are employed by a small, medium, or large business, the rules and commitment to systems thinking can be scaled to meet your size. Also, even if your company is experiencing good fortune currently, it is likely that your competitors who are studying more advanced processes which align themselves to systems thinking and processes, may be adjusting themselves to it right now.

Organizational structures vary in two primary ways, local or international. However, due to the increase of technologies, even middle-sized companies are beginning to lean more toward the international environment to stay competitive. One of the key aspects of the international shift is due to the lower cost to supply products and services through specialization and aligning systems thinking to the international and competitive processes. This seems especially true if those companies are in chained based environments.

Many multi-international companies can avoid risk by diversifying their portfolio of both costs and offerings through national and international offerings of similar products or services. It may cost less to manufacture an item in one country than another, or what sells well in one culture may not sell well in another. Also, governmental agreements associated with marketing may curtail standing operations for advertising, or certain skill sets may be available in an area that are not available in others, and so on.

Depending on which environment the organization inhabits, their cultures can also determine how their functional, matrix, product, customer, geographic cultures, and so on react to competition. Adjusting to compartmentalized decisions that support each connective opportunity is strategic. Adopting systems thinking strategies sooner, rather than later, is imperative to corporate and organizational futures to survive long-term. Also, adopting system thinking strategies will become more and more important as costs fluctuate when comparing shipping outlays versus maintaining store front access for customers and clients.

Senior managers lead middle-managers who help develop processes and manage those processes with the help of the people who get the job done. Likewise, small companies must manage personalities to fit their competitive markets with fluidity. As senior and middle-level managers of corporations, middle-sized, and even some small companies, these managers need to have strategic plans that fit those differing environments. Those environments can change rapidly. Each manager should have a baseline to shift from so that strategic goals have meaning. Unless managers are aware of some of the conceptual paths to overt business disaster and strengthen their organization's ability to withstand competition, they will have a much harder chance of shifting goals and operations necessary to survive against competitors quickly enough.

The intent of this book is to help senior managers out-maneuver their competition through learning how to adopt a systems approach to change and continuous improvement management. Second, through the parsing of successful operational segments, this book can help senior managers, middle-managers, and government/military leaders take that glut of information and parse it into the CCIM Three-Leg Stool environment. Therefore, it is not a basic business book; since so much of the baseline business concepts should be already known to fully comprehend the content.

However, these concepts are explained thoroughly enough so the undergrad through the master's college level of understanding can be applied and can be used as a tool to help build on previous experiences for better future outcomes. Also, it is not a paint-by-number rendition of how managers should complete each business step to fit their business. That goal would be unobtainable and frankly ludicrous. This is the reason why this book is important to you. Senior or middle-managers quite simply cannot read this book and not begin to see the entrepreneurial side of how systems thinking might improve their company or organization. Once managers have this reference on their bookshelf, they may want to highlight areas that they might visit from time to time as their business and leadership knowledge and environments change.

For those senior and middle-level managers who are well healed in the art of systems thinking, this book will help to further establish connected themes and operational co-dependencies within their companies and organizations until now may be currently unrealized. It will further enhance the manager's knowledge base of how the employees, across your company's or organization's spectrum, perform their group or individual operations of work-whether they are task, technical, or process oriented in nature. No longer is it acceptable, or even prudent, to believe the tasks that the senior manager believes he/she knew when managing at a lower level of responsibility are the same. They aren't. In fact, if a senior or middle-manager leaves a job and it has been 2 years since their promotion to another position, the tasks he/she completed to accomplish the jobs they vacated have changed an average of 20%. If they have left the job 5 years ago, the tasks to complete those same or like jobs have changed approximately 45 to 50%, especially if those tasks primarily interface with changes in technical fields involving their customers, suppliers, or adversaries.

Should any manager be in doubt, let me explain how this happens. At least a few of the customers, clients, and suppliers your business is involved with have changed to keep up with their own competitors. Their technologies may have changed, their methods of delivery might have changed somewhat, or their structures and priorities to do business with their own customers or suppliers may have changed. Senior or middle-managers should not ignore the scope of change, because ignoring it is a true and measurable business risk. Believing otherwise leads to the risk of your own company's obsolescence.

Chapter 1 – Intro to the CCIM Three-Leg Stool

The Change and Continuous Improvement Management (CCIM) Three-Leg Stool is a conceptual tool to be used by both middle and senior management. It is focused to improve communications and processes that are driven by the ever-changing needs of business environments. Middle-managers can use it to help them ferret out operational challenges and applications associated with changing tasks within their divisions, keep processes up to date, and keep their divisional units efficient. Senior management can use the information obtained by their middle-management to help communicate updated divisional requirements which can help point to new opportunities.

Background

Without exception the business executives I talk to agree that businesses today and those of only 10-15 years ago are vastly different. Not so much in the vision, but also in the way they must enact those visions. How the vision is communicated or secured across the organization (the who, when, and why) can either detract or contribute to both the effectiveness and the efficiencies of the organization. Associatively, the information needed to attract, retain, and solidify those visions is impacted by faster and faster technology introductions and are further exacerbated by quicker and quicker attacks from competitors. Those advances require quicker and more creative ways to deal with them. Also, the combinations of those changes increase the challenges for stakeholders, senior, and middle-management for small and medium corporations everywhere.

More and more industry leaders are at the breaking point. Many opt toward not making decisions due to those ever-increasing informational bombardments and begin to draw toward uncertainty and find themselves planning for short-term wins. While it may seem comfortable, the problem with focusing on short term wins that no longer support the long-term survivability of the company, organization, or corporation can lead to lost value and obsolescence of your product or service. Also, those senior managers who attempt to focus on the future of their companies or organizations often rely on Lean, Lean Six Sigma, ISO, Balanced Score Sheet, Best Practices, Operations Research Systems Analysis (ORSA-Army), and so on, as attempts to correct shortcomings. However, they often serve to provide limited and short-term business solutions.

Therefore, they are not the panacea of business solutions. Until these solutions are applied throughout the organization, and in a way that can be systematically sustained throughout the organization, the benefits they often yield are short-term and often fail. Additionally, a short-term focus can lead to a melancholy drive to improve the company, unsuccessful efforts to thwart competitors, and, if repeated often enough, it can enable those business planners an excuse when they are unwilling to perform. So, how do stakeholders, senior and middle-managers stay focused toward short-term wins that support long-term engagements across their organizations and corporations? This book introduces a solution.

By enhancing conceptions across the organizational whole, each challenge is separated into segments of short and long-term goals. Then the connectiveness of the segments are explained in a clear but flexible way so senior and middle-management can apply then to help make organizational and strategic decisions. The CCIM Three-Leg Stool is a concept to help explain how each leg of the Stool supports the profits, efficiencies, and effectiveness of the company while aligning the organization to a systems and continuous improvement approach that is sustainable.

Also, functional areas, depicted as legs, are supported by lateral rungs which keep the legs from shifting into resource losses and unsustainable organizational profits. Further, the CCIM Three-Leg Stool depicts ranges of flexibility enough to withstand small changes within the environments that are different for each company. It is critical that business leaders understand the inner workings of the whole of their company or organizational systems before making strategic operational decisions.

Each leg, and each supporting rung, will be described and how they interact with a continually progressive explanation of those interactions as the chapters unfold. This text can reveal how the individual parts, as part of the whole, will add to the senior and middle-managers concept of systems dynamics and how each decision can interact, adjust, or impact the other. However, it must be noted that every contingency can never be rationalized, controlled, or planned for.

When soothsayers are many, rational possibility should prevail. This book will provide some insights to provide an individualized strategic planning direction to go forward, and then offer some guidance towards the depth for which it must occur, to remain competitive. Further, it will enhance communication between your company's management teams as they explore the reason for co-dependent communications, both in functional and operational structures, across your organization. As depicted by Engle (2013) and supported by Saberton (2018) when approached this way, both independent silos and group think intertwine to support corporate profits and long-term sustainability.

Chapter 2 – Employees

The total number of individuals employed, or attempting to be employed, in the U.S. civilian labor force has and will continue to have significant changes in both scope and demographic make-up. These significant changes are broader than they have been over the previous half of the 20th century. According to Toossi (2013), the Census Bureau's 2012 population projections through 2022 denoted that the U.S. population is expected to continue to grow gradually, to grow older, and to become more racially and culturally diverse. Their 2018 through 2028 projections depict that older workers, over 65, will stay in the workforce longer. They will assuage the employment gaps of younger workers, ages 16 to 24, which are decreasing as that age demographic is staying in schools longer. That means how employers communicate, interact, and involve those diverse workforce groups will also require revisional aspects to keep up and retain the best employees to meet the requisites of future company and organizational health.

Employees need more than a paycheck, especially for future employees. [See Table 1]. The old form and ideas of employers enjoying life-long employees is almost dead. Why? A little over a decade ago many companies experienced downsizing, reorganizations, and diversification of their operational and financial portfolios. Also, the overall company operations were not as hampered with rapid change due to the onslaught associated with their individual environments. These environments included the government, taxes, competition, and the technology boom all of which only exacerbated those challenges.

While technological enhancements are growing, the outlook for individuals who wish to work is downsizing. According to CareerBuilder (2018) more than 1 in 5 employees reported that they expect to change jobs during the latter half of 2018. According to Pendell (2018), 51% of the U.S. workforce are vigorously looking for other employment. Further, as reported by the U.S. Dept of Labor (2018), median employee longevity for males was 4.3 years, and 4.0 for females. Therefore, the requirement to provide for future employees, who need to see the organization they work for as a stepping stone to higher skills and learning, has become increasingly necessary.

Pendell (2018) believed leading employees to help them see how their future successes are incorporated into what they learn from your company and how their affiliation with your organization will lead them to higher wages and a higher standard of living loom prominently in making choices of where to apply for work. It has become more important than it was only a few short years ago. Also, they are less likely to have the patience to wait as long as those in the past for that training which can lead to their future advancement.

Associatively, HR professionals must incorporate changes to their overall employee recruitment and schema of training and retention programs. Soliciting employees and keeping employees are two separate parts which should work in tandem to obtain a common organizational goal.

Subsequently, companies must be sure they can live up to any hype on-boarding systems or that those in management create when advertising employee opportunities. In today's environment, communication between perspective and current employees is quick and unfiltered. Impressions, whether factual or impulsively derived, are carried via the internet to your perspective public almost instantaneously. These instantaneous impressions are also used by your current employees. Therefore, senior managers should review their current on-boarding processes and incorporate backward planning to ferment the goal of employee retention. This should occur before the beginning of the on-boarding processes.

Further, according to Pendell (2018), only 12% of current workers intensely agree that the companies they work for do an impressive job of hiring employees. When on-boarding employees, your current employees believe those working in the human resource (HR) areas focus primarily on the proper paperwork and not on supporting your company's distinctive culture. The information they receive leaves the perspective employees asking what is expected of them. If the prospective hire does not understand his or her role in your company, it is much harder for them to see working for your company in the long-term.

It has been my experience that this oversight is often duplicated in reality. Younger workers evaluate what they might learn to further their future careers when seeking employment. Most of the younger employees I talk to state that they understand they may not stay at a company in the long-run, so it is important to learn what they can from the job they are in currently. So, making ongoing training part of the job will increase in its importance, because they believe if they are to stay at a company longer, it means the training they receive must also be transferable once they leave.

Subsequently, part of HR's procedures should include ways for employees to ferment the training and experiences they get at their current job into advancements towards future employment. Do this even if you believe they won't stay with your company or organization. Why? It is easy to become complacent and become comfortable with not training at all, especially if the only goal is to procure a short-term means to an end for the company. Otherwise, management decisions could contribute to the revolving door of rehiring younger employees when you may not need to. If for no other reason to adopt this strategy is the realization that - not training them is worse, if they stay with your company!

Also, when using this lens and applying these procedures to study the worker and sustainable employee futures, it is easier to see how the skills your organization provides will transfer to other vocations. Those skills will transfer in most cases. Rampton (2017) believed younger employees like organization, constancy, adaptable work schedules, benefits such as telecommuting, appreciation from the supervisor, bonuses, stock, and gift cards as monetary incentives, instant feedback, and continuous learning occasions. Selling your company's benefits will begin to look more lucrative to future young employees, because the skills enhancements offered represents a part of the overall *likes* of newer employees.

Further, employees want to feel they are listened to and heard. They don't want to be just a member of a gripe session within the company. They want their bosses to acknowledge them and the work they do. Most do not want a constant pat on the back, but they do want to know their ideas are at least considered. They can accept that much better than not being heard, at all. If their ideas are not timed well, won't work yet, or is a bridge too far for the company, they want to know it. Further, as posited by Ben-Porat (1981), employees wish to have a degree of control and responsibility for their jobs and their professional development. Tie those concepts together into processes and procedures, provide manager training that postulates more positive relations with those they interface or work with, and add a positive and an equitable rewards system which allows feedback to the employee. A military (Marine) vernacular is particular useful here: "Adapt and Overcome". When all else seems to fail, do what works best and understand the *why*. Teaching the *why* makes it much easier should management need to readjust a process or procedure in the future.

One of the best ways to achieve a more productive and satisfied work force is to build employee satisfaction through work policy and processes. Policy and processes are the parents to the procedures that follow. As children, procedures must align and support the parents. If they are not reviewed, preferably by an outside entity or change agent over time, those alignments may not support one another. Further, when the policies, processes, and procedures do not align, the costs can be higher than expected. As explained by McDermott, Spence-Lashinger, and Shamian, (1996) who completed studies involving nurses in part to deter employee turn-over, it is important to build success into the process of work. To build successes into the processes of work, more than a cursory review of what must be done to complete a job satisfactory should be reviewed periodically and should involve each job description.

Job satisfaction decreases, when job descriptions do not align with job procedures to get work accomplished. Job dissatisfaction relates directly to job turnover. Associatively, according to Pendell, (2018) 51% of presently employed adults admit they are investigating new job opportunities. Opportunities to grow and job flexibilities that permit life-style adjustments and expand their abilities top the list to retain them. Human resource managers might add to their set of skills their abilities to have constant contact with employee opinions, attitudes, and their emotions, because worker dissatisfaction leads to several organizational losses more than simply the loss of the employee.

Further, the expectations of the job and the job procedures need to match closely enough so that annual performance reviews reward alignment with the company goals. This alignment is associated with more than an administrative review. Overall, when a pragmatic review is accomplished, it must provide hope for the employee that they can do better.

As stated by Pendell (2018), only 14% of workers are convinced their annual reviews motivate them to do better. Also, less than 33% have faith that their annual reviews are just and accurate. One reason the annual employee reviews continually miss the mark is the rapid change of business itself. Employee reviews are happening too infrequently. Today, it is much quicker for annual reviews to reach obsolescence because those reviews simply may not make sense by the time managers and employees discuss them. This only exacerbates the challenge of employees not seeing themselves working at your company for the long-term and increases opportunities for employee turnover.

We have sometimes seen turn-over treated as a secondary consideration to business success. Realistically, the impact of turn-over will vary with the type of company or organization, and those that lead them. Regardless of how frustrating it may seem to some within management, the human element will remain important even if to check the reliability or calibrate the machines that complete repetitive work. Overlooking considerable turn-over within such companies or organizations is contrary to long-term survival and strategic successes.

Sometimes managers do not consider the total costs of individuals, or groups of individuals, hired with a pragmatic eye of total costs, i.e. – the hiring cost, the hidden training costs (often it involves others already trained to help the new employees when helping to train them procedures). Terminating an employee might not be the best first option, when comparing and contrasting the costs associated with re-training or moving the employee, who at least has an idea of the organizational culture, is an alternative.

The administrative costs to rehire are often known, but only when a close examination of the total costs is reviewed for a determination of a possible termination, it becomes more realistic. Figure 1 depicts many

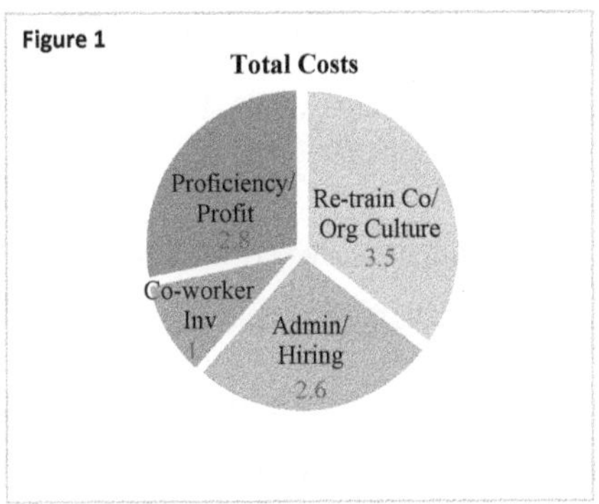

of the over-looked costs to such decisions. There are at least four costs associated with the hiring of a new employee. First, Re-train the company's organizational culture is represented by the time it takes to inculcate the new worker to understand and act as part of the company team. It takes time to indoctrinate the new employee to the culture of the organization. Interacting with other employees, what the company stands for, and so on can affect loyalty, readiness, and retention. Second, Proficiency and Profit represent the time to learn how to complete all the tasks of the job. Proficiencies leading to profit can be short, or longer, depending on the tasks and level of the job. Third, Administration and Hiring represents the administrative and people tasks associated with every new hire. Finally, Co-worker Involvement, represents the level that co-workers must involve themselves with helping the new hires learn the *when*, *why*, and *how* those jobs are to be done satisfactorily. This represents lost time and lost effort as co-workers must step away from their own responsibilities to help. How those decisions are communicated and absorbed by the current workforce also represent costs.

Company human resources (HR) leaders and organizational managers often discuss the differences in motivations for different individuals. As posited by Tope (2017), how management relations become part of the culture and how managers adjudicate their own leadership styles with the different needs of their employees matter. As an example, depending on the jobs to be accomplished, lower-level task or higher-level relationship oriented, the employee relationship might be different. The job task may require high efficiency and quality and the employee might actually want prescribed directions to achieve those high efficiency tasks. Or, another employee might be given the latitude to utilize creative talents to perform customer relations work that requires flexibility on an as needed basis.

The task-oriented manager may provide exacting steps to be accomplished, while the over-sight manager might suggest ways to improve jobs that improve the overall relational operations focused to advance internal or external cooperativeness. Either type of management style works, if both the knowledge and motivation fit the job. The best managers know when and who to develop so that task-oriented jobs and those jobs that require employee latitude match the management influence so that motivation is a self-reciprocating standard. Whether the employee is in a task-oriented job, or is an employee with more latitudes to make decisions, the employees may require different ways to influence them.

However, task-oriented and over-sight job managements are not the only leadership styles to consider when motivating employees. Watching how individual employees react to situations reveal how they think over time. The employee who thinks centrally has a broader sense of the organization, compared to an employee who thinks de-centrally, and each has a different way to conceptualize work itself. This concept is supported by Kearns (2012), who believed that not studying how those motivations can be most effectively engendered so that an efficient work ethic is enjoyed by the company, can be detrimental. His study indicated that those who acted with a centric mindset had tendencies to use their title to help their individual earnings compared to helping the organization to coordinate and share information. While those that thought with a de-centralized mind-set were more likely to engage in organizational activities that help engender relationships and trust. Also, while research is still broadening concerning mindsets and ability or inability to integrate into the current and future workforce, the challenges associated with age groups and cultural wants of employees are available for consideration.

Cultures

After on-boarding employees, the matriculation of the policies, processes, and procedures should be included to encompass different age and ethnic groups. Each age or ethnic group represents cultures which are different from one another. The following examples posited by the Glassdoor Team (2016) suggested how benefits packages might be designed to help attract and retain different employees within different cultural groups.

Building benefits packages with a focus to manage and retain employees must appeal to different generations and represent only slices of the skills the HR managers must know. The other is knowing how to retain those employees of different cultures and mindsets. Managers and stakeholders should endeavor to know the width and depth of their current and future workforce populations.

We can now address how age groups and general studies help to confirm the wants and needs of generational groups. Although the dates to categorize the different generations of the workforce vary, I follow the orientations and forecasts as explained by Kasasa (2020) which are: *Baby Boomers*: Born between the mid-1940s and mid-1960s; *Gen Xers*: Born between the mid-1960s through 1980; *Millennials*: Born between early 1980s and mid-1990s; and *Gen Zers*: Born between the mid-1990s through 2015.

As explained by Toossi (2015), many Baby Boomers will exit the workforce by 2020; however, the 55 and older workers replacing them will grow from 21.7 per cent (2014) of the workforce to 25% by 2024. Also, as described by the U.S. Department of Labor-Bureau of Labor Statistics (2017), every Baby Boomer will be the age of 65 or greater by the year 2030. At that time, 1 in every 5 individuals in the U.S. will be of retirement age. Further, according to the U.S. Census Bureau (2018) by the year 2034 individuals over 65 years of age are estimated to outnumber those who are under 18 years old for the very first time.

Using a rolling scale to extrapolate findings for the below will also help understand these statistics. People will age and leave the workforce at differing rates in the future. According to Toossi (2016), the Baby Boomer (henceforth, Boomer) employees will begin to decrease to around 22% of the workforce by 2060. So, plans to utilize the Boomer workforce as mentors for younger employees might be a good option.

As posited by Quick Take-Catalyst (2018) and Ratanjee (2018), Millennials will represent 75%, of the global workforce by 2025. Further, they will be the largest contributors to fill vacancies associated with the retiring Boomers (Pew Research, 2018).

Generalities are a good guide for management to consider, but it is the wisest of managers who can see past the stereotypical and find the employee that straddles those generalizations. They will be the employees that will help management adjust the workforce because they will know both sides of the cultural gaps. [See Table 1]. These general cultural gaps exist. As posited by Schawbel (2017), generally, Boomers appreciate a good salary level, want medical insurance, 60% of them look for occupations that have meaningful work and 57% the job location must fit their life situations.

According to Fry (2017), Generation-Xers appreciate a good salary level, a 401K plan with corresponding benefits, job stability, promotion opportunities, and schedules that are more personalized to match their lifestyle. According to the U.S. Bureau of Labor Statistics (2018), approximately 63% of workers in the Gen-X population are employed.

Also, according to Schawbel (2017) and Rampton (2017), Millennials appreciate benefits alternatives, paid time off, the capability to work off-site, and flexible work schedules. Millennials are generally more educated and independent, considered by some to be the indulged generation, need recognition and consideration for accomplishments, highly connected, need instant gratification and focusing on productivity is best, need individual career advancement, want job flexibility in schedules, and want work-life balance. They want to work with capable people and appreciate two-way mentorships. The Millennial's work effort is broad enough in scope that it can affect the entire company, and they typically do not like cynicism.

According to Alton (2017), generally, Millennials do not like to talk on the phone and prefer email, texting, or messaging. This may clash with other generational groups who prefer face-to-face over more technological devices. [See Chap 7]. Management might encourage them to improve their communication skills, and could set up rewards to achieve that improvement.

Further, according to Sammer (2018), generation Zers want financial planning assistance, fitness memberships, identify with web solutions, and support from mentors. Generation Z are generally the most connected to technology, are creative and entrepreneurial, driven to impact society, and requires competitive salaries if hired. As posited by Inc. (2019) they will make up about 24% of the global workforce by 2020.

As technology increases (Bartels, 2017), these future employees will inculcate these changes and help managers train their divisional employees and peers to use them. However, to retain these employees, managers should learn what will keep them employed with and within [See Engaged versus Dis-Engaged] your company. To keep them, management could offer to support their entrepreneurial mindsets, clearly lay out their possible future within the company, and offer to support networking with them for the sake of your company. Also, Generation Zer's will help the Millennials fill in the gap for the retiring Boomers as more enter the workforce in 2020.

Table 1 **Age/Primary Benefits Interest** **Forecast 2024/2025**

	Meaningful Work	Life Situations	Good Salary	Medical Ins	401K	Job Stability	Promo Ops	Job2 Flex	Fin/Plan Asst	Fitness Memb	Mentor Spt
Gen Z	R							R			R
Millennials	R	S				SR	S	SR			R
Gen X		F	F		FR	F	FR	R			R
Baby Boomers	S	S	SR	S			R				

Source entries are: Fry (F), Rampton (R), and Schawbel (S).

Note: Credible age agreement between Gen Z and Millennials are mixed, therefore they are combined.

Managing employees from different age groups requires practice. As posited by Wisdom (2019), when employees from different cultures are part of the decision-making process of a company or an organization, they will have different concepts of how to complete actions associated with technologies and customer satisfaction. Bringing different age groups to the decision table will simply bring a more diverse set of decision skills and processes to it. At first, bringing these age combinations to the decision table may send up red flags to less seasoned management facilitators, but the outcomes can be impressive. According to Lin (2019), managing the age differences through and the understanding of individual abilities can improve communication; which builds better cultures and organizational futures. Also, mixing age groups broadens your organization's ability to serve customers and clients who are also of mixed age groups. So, mixing the groups with ages and skill sets in mind, is a good management tool. [See Chap 5].

Such ideas are supported by La Loggia (2018), concerning how focusing on skill sets that complement one another within the group decreases the cultural aspect. When managers decrease the cultural aspects of projects, they become less of an obstacle. Also, allowing leaders to emerge given their skills and opinions within their relative strengths will further diminish the concern for age differences.

As management increases their skills of mixing subordinate managers and employee project groups, some stagnation may begin to occur. Should that happen, or if the skill sets begin to stale, re-mix part of the group and skill sets. Further, the mixing of age groups provides cultural cross training and should help to provide solutions that will fit wider diverse situations and projects. The more management knows what motivates the different generations to work best, they will know how to keep them engaged doing the work required to be efficient. [See Chap 8].

Common challenges in these differentiated groups are represented by disagreements associated with advancement opportunities, work proficiency, and technology. As described by Benjamin (2019), older employees tend to focus on quality while younger employees will focus on efficiencies. Harmonizing them is important in today's competitive markets. Customers and clients will want value added to offerings in products and services, as higher quality technologies change.

Also, a fairly common struggle for managers is allowing themselves to stereotype individuals simply by the employees associated age group, initially. As explained by Fuhl (2019), instead, first look at the individual skills and individual attributes of the employee and then apply them to the general knowledge of their generation. Each individual will bring a skill another will not have, so understanding those skills and putting them to work for the benefit of the team and company is important. Collaboration between the generations, which focus on the optimization of skill sets can build trust and openness where conflicts associated with shortfalls will not. A focused outcome aimed at the benefit of the company can help decrease biased generalizations between age groups. Also, the variations within them might allow differing levels of management to have the opportunity for those employee variations to be seen as strengths. Once managers are trained to utilize these management skills and tactics, those age group differences can become more valued than they were previously.

Further, and as posited by the U.S. Department of Labor-Bureau of Labor Statistics (2017), the racial and ethnic makeup of companies are changing rapidly. Asians and Hispanics are projected to increase much quicker than the average annual rates of other employees from 2016 to 2026, 2.5 % and 2.7 %, respectively. By 2026 Hispanic employees are expected to represent 1 out of 5 employees in the workforce. Further, according to the U.S. Department of Labor-Bureau of Labor Statistics (2018), the black workforce will increase from the 2016 totals of 12.3% of the workforce to 12.7% of the workforce in 2026. As the age, ethnic, and racial makeup of the workforce continues to change, so will the requirements to keep employees engaged in the workplace.

Engaged versus dis-engaged

Employee engagement and burnout are associated. If employees feel engaged in their work, they enjoy it; however, if they feel engaged and valued less burnout occurs. In a study conducted by Asplund and Leibbrandt, et al. (2020), they indicated that strengths, well-being, and engagement reduce employee stress. Further, Pendell (2018) agreed that productivity dollars are lost, as 63% of those employees who are burned-out tend to take more sick days and of those 23% tend to go to the emergency room. Further, keeping employees from becoming burned-out can make a positive impact on retention, aspirations for career enhancements, and improves the employee's family lives.

Also, engagement seems to be connected to employee's perception of using their individual strengths in the workplace. Rigoni, Asplund, and Sorenson (2014) indicated that 56% of adult employees state they only use their individual strengths for six hours or less every day. Improving those statistics only strengthen engagement, because those with perceptions of using their individual strengths are more productive, have higher self-possession, are happier, have higher prospects, and promote more selflessness.

Further, how employees react to their working environment is different for the engaged and dis-engaged worker is also important. Engaged workers, those that actively and emotionally participate in the workplace create value added to their work. Dis-engaged workers increase friction among their peers and customers. As explained by Harter, Agrawal, S., and Sorenson (2014), 13% of global workers are engaged in the workplace, 63% do not engage themselves in the workplace, and 24% are vigorously dis-engaged. Also, losses associated with the lack of workplace engagement rob companies and organizations of resources which are often not perceived immediately, but instead show as productivity losses on the bottom line each year. Not only is it important to focus on the loss of those resources throughout the year, but also it is important to understand these losses exist and learning how to overcome them are important. Those lost profits can prevent companies from using those resources to enhance their competitiveness in the marketplace. If your work environment is similar, the company is losing money!

Associatively, a study published a year earlier by Sorenson and Garman (2013), there are differences in work engagement between ages in the workplace within the United States. They state that Traditionalists (born 1945 or before) are engaged with the work to be accomplished 41% of the time. Millennials were engaged 33% of the time. Those Millennials who were actively engaged want to find other jobs only 17% of the time compared to 50% of the time when compared to those who are actively disengaged. Retaining the largest group of the workforce will require companies to engage them and give them occasions to gather the skills to grow. Therefore, boosting engagement is becoming more important to keeping both current and future employees.

On average, 30% of Gen Xers and 28% of Millennials are engaged in the workplace compared to 31% of Boomers and 38% of Traditionalists. [See Table 2]. A study conducted by Harter and Agrawal (2014) for United States workers, indicated that these figures change slightly for boomers, who want to retire after age 65, but remain more engaged.

One of the reasons Boomers are retiring later may be because they are not confident that they will have enough money to do what they wish to do after retiring. As depicted by the Englund (2020), Boomers worry about their retirement including concerns that retirement ages continue to move and the changing definition of retirement itself. Boomers have approximately 20% less in savings, 20% lower household wealth, and 100% more debt than the traditionalists before them.

Traditional workers have similar challenges to Boomers when retirement age occurs. As explained by Purcell (2000), for traditional workers retirement used to mean stop working and draw pension benefits immediately. More and more traditional workers and employers opt for phased retirement or retirement plans that offer 401k time employee inducements. Offering benefit programs that fit worker situations help to keep employees engaged. The differences between global

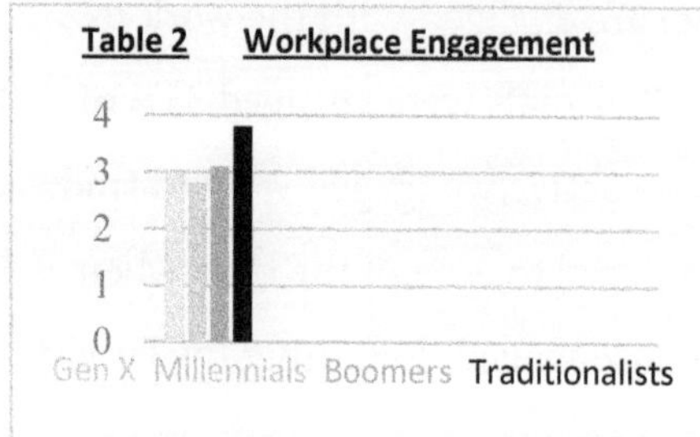

engagement and engagement studies for the United States employees alone are substantial. Further, how study developers define age groupings, which vary slightly, can change these figures marginally, but are also closely related enough to give us tools to plan the how we help to develop improvements in engagement.

Further, keeping the workforce engaged and productive means understanding not only how to manage the different age groups, but also leading them into the future. As posited by DeLong (2017), who believed this means stimulating and keeping impatient Millennials engaged, provide advancement training for Gen-Xers, and capitalizing on the productivity of Boomers before their upcoming retirement will prove to be a wise investment for your organization.

Part-time and Gig

As the workforce changes, both demographically and culturally, another segment of workers should be considered. The part-time and gig (project) workers represent much of the current workforce in matrixed organizations. In this case, matrixed organizations are those that have both full-time and part-time workers. Gandhi (2018) posited that matrixed organizations make up 84% of workers. Also, managers who manage employee flex-time should know that 51% of employees would break away from their current jobs to attain flex-time. Subsequently, finding ways to leverage outsourced employees is becoming more important.

Workers who work as matrixed-employees have challenges which include the need to know what prioritizations are first and how not to lose their productivity because of requirements to attend several meetings due to the diversification of their managers. Gig workers (those who work for various companies to perform a task or service with definitive ends or having a terminal result) represent 36% of those in the matrixed workforce. While there exists overlap between the matrixed and gig workers, gig workers experience challenges with dis-association with the company due to non-inclusion with the internal social environment. As an example, some employees work from their homes or through other third-party entities.

Management should ask themselves if the part-time or gig workers are treated, trained, and offered possible opportunities the same as regular workers? Are communication channels, individual development, and relationships equitably dispersed to the part-time or gig workers from the management? Feeling a part of an organization and believing in what that organization's benefits might be, add to the retention of both internal and external employees. Employee retention and how it is achieved is championed by Gandhi (2018), who submitted that a company's development platform is typically created for the general employee population; however, a professional development platform is personal for employees. Looking for shortfalls in such areas represents a primary difference between managing projects and leading people.

Chapter 3 – Equipment and Technology

Equipment scalability, both in physical size and production ability, will continue to change as technological advances provide new opportunities for companies and organizations to remain competitive. Global sales predictions of technology software, IT hardware, and the services provided to organizations and governmental agencies will only increase. In fact, Gownder, Le Clair, Martorelli, et al. (2019) foresaw automation to lead digital transformations influencing everything from organizations through the customer to operational corporate models. Although manufacturing may quickly come to mind, technological growth will increase in virtually all categories of business.

While some technology-based organizations and companies (examples: IBM, NASA, etc.) experienced rapid technological growth, most did not. In general, that is no longer true. According to Bartels (2017) and projected by Gowdner, Clair, et al. (2018), worldwide purchases of technology software, hardware, and services by businesses and governments grew by 3.4% in 2017, and by 4% in

2018. New projections by Le Clair (2020) suggest that technological solutions will displace 16% of workers by 2030. Subsequently, not only are today's businesses experiencing rapid change, but also the environment in which those rapid business changes occur is rapidly changing especially in technological areas.

Equipment and technology are not the only drivers which promote the profitability scale. Your customers and clients, do! If you know your customers and their wants and needs, management can help shape the processes and procedures that provide those requirements better. In fact, without the customers and clients that drive business requirements, the equipment and technologies must, by order of precedence alone, fall to the second tier of business capabilities.

A possible example might go like this, imagine sending your chief mechanical director to a conference of new technological breakthroughs which the senior manager believes align with your manufacturing plant. He/she comes back with a new idea for equipment upgrades or new equipment that is faster and less costly than repairing the old equipment. The upgrade equipment does essentially the same thing, only quicker. Sounds good, so far.

Now let's look at the overall reality of the situation. Your recent survey of your customers reveal they want a higher quality product, and your competitor is providing it at the same price as your business. Senior managers have an obligation to adjust to stay competitive. So, the new equipment idea doesn't sound bad. Then, management discovers the quality will remain the same. Not a good swap. That only means the company will be making products with no higher quality faster. Management must find another option.

Historically, and according to Hamel and Prahalad (1996), the significance is apparent when components of your business are evaluated side by side with your competitor's products or services. If a company discounts their competitors, even if you are in the lead currently, it can be damaging. Your consumers vote with their feet and their wallet.

As promoted by Sanow (2013), most of your customers and clients vie for more convenience, value added, and the quality of your relationships with them. Your customers' positive experiences require a perpetual review of your products or services and how they compare to your competitors. Associatively, those positive experiences help produce long-term and relational successes. The review, customer education, and upgrade of products and services, provided through operations and process analysis, marketing and advertising, and R&D help to keep customers satiated and competitors at bay.

Despite what some may say, not everything old is bad and not everything new is good and vice versa. Also, a better warranty policy or a better service rendered from either a legacy or newer idea may provide your customers an improved experience. So, where should your company start? Senior managers could start by reviewing and analyzing your industry, and where it is going.

From that point evaluate where your company is currently, then adjust pragmatically. As supported by Forbes Technology Council (2018), senior managers might start with finding out what your suppliers, vendors, or clients use for equipment or technologies. As examples: Management need not announce to the world your internal processes, but public relation managers might explain why your overall processes produce a better experience for the customer or client. [See Chap 5]. Also, when contemplating the purchase of new equipment or repairing existing equipment, costs should be compared for each, but if either your old equipment turns out a better product or your old policy provides a better value added for your customers, keep them and let your customers know it. The danger here is becoming lazy about researching other product and value-added options your company can offer current and future customers. This can happen to any company that has experienced maturity and has become complacent in their product offerings.

Such understanding was not lost on Garry Ridge, President/CEO of WD-40, concerning a product that had been well known by its customers. Stagnation of the brand awareness led to losses in sales and market shares. Ridge (2018), reinvigorated the company by leading the company's managers and employees to focus on how both conceptualized their jobs.

> "Learning moments can be positive or negative, but they are never bad, so long as they are shared for the benefit of all."
>
> \- Garry Ridge

He developed a learning organization in the sense of creativity, with its associated risks, and was rewarded when people increased their respective ownership for their jobs. The openness across the organization allowed for interpersonal respect among his employees. Employees who were otherwise more competitive individually became more focused and began creating product variability that met the needs of the WD-40 customer base, and beyond.

Such examples help prove that cost-effective choices associated with equipment and technology should not only make work easier for your employees, but also can lead to a more diverse set of product and service offerings to your customers. Understandably, they also must have an ROI for the purchase of that equipment or technology which makes sense for the company. The civilian and military considerations for matching equipment and technologies are analogous in the sense that the needs of the customer (civilian, governmental, and military members) should meet the needs and the uses for the combinations of equipment, technologies, and human operators. [See Chapter 10]. These integrative solutions vary, and each requires individual comparisons and contrasts. For civilian markets many of these solutions are derived from the civilian marketplace analysis with combinations of acquired technologies and R&D. The military might incorporate branch specific programs which apply concepts that employ knowledge of human systems integration (HSI).

While it may seem that military organizations do not have competitors, other than a foreign enemy, they do. As an example, Ukman (2011) reported that Robert Gates, then the Secretary of Defense, closed USJFCOM in 2011 due in part to the U.S. budget constraints, the effectiveness of overall training compared to other commands, and so on. Such occasions, remind us that all aspects of the operations must align to be efficient and effective. Because competitors exist, it is essential that the human elements must align with the diversification of the equipment, the span of the customers supplied, and in this case the military branches or international environments in which the organization operates.

If the span of customers is small, generally less diversification is needed – but also considerations for more localized competitors should still be a concern. International configurations of the equipment may mean a new set of tools and maintenance schedules for the same types of equipment might be needed. Additionally, some countries may require the manufacturing or processing equipment be purchased in their country, before accepting the gaining company's purchase order to acquire the equipment to set up the business. Or, in the case of North Atlantic Treaty Organization's (NATO) oversight with the U.S. Army's U.S. 21st TAACOM - Combat Equipment Group Europe (CEGE), which required that a certain number of Dutch employees were represented with a mixture of U.S. equipment maintainers of Pre-positioned Material Configured to Unit Sets (POMCUS) combat equipment.

Each situation requires negotiations to permeate operations that meet competitive challenges. Regardless of either the span or diversification challenges any company or organization currently experience, their competitors will change either as a whole or when they diversify their offerings to customers or clients. The equipment and technologies combine to equip employees to accomplish the tasks assigned. Staying abreast of these changes requires periodic reviews and that is not slowing down. According to Forrester (2017), global purchases of technology software, hardware, and services by companies and governments will continue to change and grow through the foreseeable future. It is a normal occurrence, and the rate and types of technology will change for each industry, but the thing that is certain is - it will change.

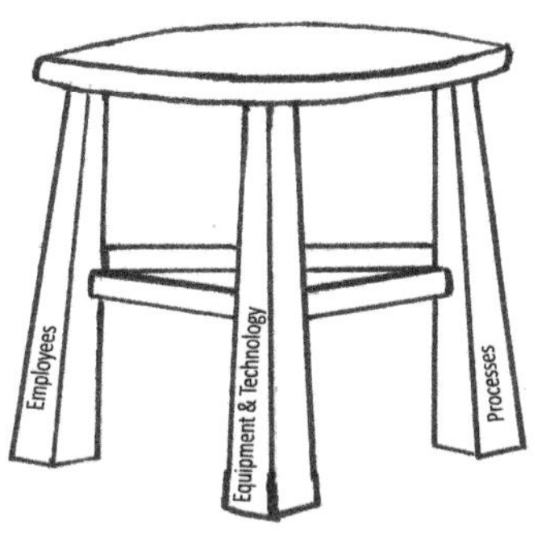

Chapter 4 – Policies, Processes, and Procedures

After years of business consulting experience, I sometimes get amazed when I talk to managers who have been promoted within the company. Some of those same managers state to me that they know everything their employees must do to complete their jobs. Regardless of how efficient they were in their position, even if fairly recently vacated, that is mostly untrue. Some may know much, but how their recently vacated job gets accomplished will change, even if the job descriptions remain static. [See Forward].

After nearly 30 years of comparing job descriptions in companies and organizations, our experiences have shown us an interesting set of data. [This is so important, it bears repeating]. In a shorter time than is usually realized, the tasks to complete those same job description activities have changed. The situation is fairly universal and has to happen. After a period of two years, the person taking his/her place has had to change *the way the job is done* approximately 20%. After a period of 5 years that same person will have to *change the way they now do the job between 45-50%*! [See

Forward]. The latter figure is especially significant if the jobs are technical in nature.

When management really examines why these changes must occur, it makes sense. There are several technological solutions for systems management software. We will focus here on the ability of organizational or systems software that maximize patching capabilities with internal differences in IT platforms across the enterprise or organization. Internal patches to facilitate change and improvement efforts are one thing, but also evaluating how these patches might integrate with your supply sources, customers, and off-site operations requires an individual effort for your organization. Each integration, internally or externally – or both, aimed to increase communication procedures or processes means alignments must occur to remain efficient. Also, the more technical your supported or supporting organizations are, the larger the change in how employees must change to adapt to accomplish the same job as in years previous.

Subsequently and rationally, both the suppliers and the customer organizations your company is connected to have changed in some, or possibly, in several different ways. Their organizational structure itself, their technologies, their distribution channels, and so on may have evolved. That means the way your company's employees may have to support, or be supported by them, must change too. Many managers do not think of this often enough. This can be a mistake. If the way employees must change to do the same job after a period of time goes unnoticed, the duplication of effort across the organization can be multiplicative and costly.

The alignment of policies, processes, and procedures help to continually ferret out those challenges, if managed properly. As posited by Kaplan and Norton (2006), strategy maps and balanced score cards may help align business units so they support one another, but also each managerial decision should support the overall strategy. Even though senior and middle-managers of business, and graduate business students have learned about vision, policy, processes, and procedures in company trainings and advanced classwork, they probably have not thought of how all these systemic business efforts conceptualize into the provisioning and professionalization of their respective organizations. They can do it. It is simply because they haven't been trained to think that way.

While there still exists some dissention between aspects of organizational guidance statements, let us agree on the following for the sake of conceptual consistently.

- Vision: Provides for the most *generalized guidance* for the company or organization. It is the attempt to capture the overarching spirit and hopes for the corporate mission or codified policies to follow.
- Policies: Further peal down responsibilities and represents the *strategic* efforts that are focused to support and attain the vision. The policies should represent how each large unit of the company or organization can support the vision. Example: The corporate policy is to serve all the customers and clients in a way that is both expedient and provides value added products or services by ……..
- Processes: Represents the *organizational* means to provide support for the policies. As posited by Kaplan and Norton (2006), expertise can be lost in the process piece of any

transition, especially if what was once a parameterized product or service becomes broad in scope. [See Figure 2]. The processes for each subordinate corporate unit might be something like: For the application in the customer experience section - all orders will be shipped to the customers/clients within 48 hours of receiving orders, and shipments will utilize the most economical and direct method for the customer/client.

- Procedures: The *tactical* operations that support the processes of the organization. The procedures represent actions that the individual units or individual positions which or who perform tasks to support the processes which are lain out by policies. Example: For customer experience section – check for incoming orders hourly, batch incoming orders by type, call production operations to alert them of batched items for processing hourly. OR - Example: For stamping area - inspect press so that 220 degrees shows up on the display before work, lay plastic and rubber mold in frame assuring that mold is seated before beginning heated press work, etc., lay finished work in cooling bin for QC inspection within 25 minutes of start time.

We have found that procedures get lost in the transition quite readily when smaller businesses or organizations transform into larger scaled entities. Often, the expertise that was once concentrated became too diverse without the infrastructure to support it. The policies, processes, and procedures are equally important and without any one of them supporting the other, alignment does not exist. Changes can occur in one unit of your company, or in several simultaneously. However, non-realized changes can cause discombobulations with efforts to provide the best customer experiences and damaging to customer relationships.

This oversight can also become apparent to your employees who notice that the customers they serve are not as satisfied as they once were. According to Pendell (2018), only 26% of workers agree that their company consistently keeps its assurances to customers. The resources required and how those resources are to be used in the most effective and efficient way, directly affects what the current customer experiences are and what future customers deliberate when choosing a product or service.

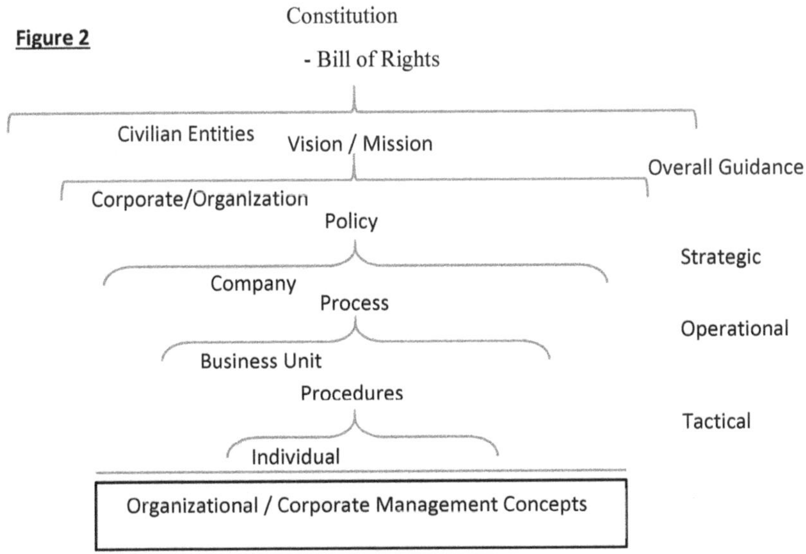

Policy, processes, and procedures…representing the strategic, operational, to tactical are all important. Policies are the parent of processes. Processes exist at the heart of *any and all* types of businesses. Business processes anchor business operational triad continuities. According to Richardson (2007), an organization's processes act as the hub for focusing resources and providing strategic guides toward commercial undertakings, the customer experiences, and expanding profit-making avenues within your marketplace. Procedures, which follow processes, intersect directly through employee activities and affect the bottom line of the business statement.

Given these links, managers should be concerned about the long-term health of their organization and periodic analysis of the links between processes and job descriptions. A pragmatic analysis between these links can reveal duplications of effort that can rob company resources and may reduce the organizational abilities to improve customer experiences. Further, the profits lost due to the duplication of effort, the mis-interpretation of communication which can lead to confusion, loss of trust, and loss of resources through inefficient processes can bankrupt a company or organization in the long run.

I have yet to find any organization, (company, corporation, civilian or military organization, profit, or non-profit entity) that has not experienced some resource losses due to inadequate review of policy, processes, and procedures. Each occurrence depletes resources that might otherwise be utilized to help improve, grow, or sustain their operations. That is another reason why each leg of the Stool must contribute to the successes of the other two so that long-term successes are reached. [See Chapter 2]. Also, what is good for one division may not be good for another in each of the three-leg CCIM categories. For now, we should realize that the indirect inputs of human predispositions associated with understanding their job description, technological interfaces, and the processes associated with them predicate how efficiently the jobs are performed.

> "If we go out of business, it will not be because we're not focused on the Internet. It will be because we're too focused on the Internet."
> - Bill Gates

Technology provides the interconnectedness between the types of management structure and individual unit structures. According to Ghosh et al. (2019), when aligned and combined properly, technologies can provide the organization improved efficiencies over their competitors. However, sharing technologies across the organization without human inputs associated with requirements and capabilities can cause distinctive discontinuities between them. Some managers may focus too much on not having enough technology. Technology, although important, may not be the problem. How to share that technology and train to reach their capabilities, may be the sticking point.

Company or organizational sharing of needed information using enhanced technology can be cross-integrated into the protection, safety, and efficiency considerations. Technology may help structure the organization, but people run it. That means human processes must be part of the organizational policy, processes, and procedures. [See Chap 2].

Procedures can be administrative or operational. Updating them and keeping them current can keep your business or organization from losing employees or losing resources. This is sometimes due to repeated actions, resultant of codification or physical actions, that need not be repeated while completing the myriad of steps as work gets accomplished. For example: As reported by Patrick and Sundaram (2018), professionals appraise that the expense, when losing an employee,_is somewhere from 1.5-2 times a worker's yearly salary to tens of thousands of dollars depending on their influence in the workplace. Administrative processes that could help alleviate those losses, when properly executed are exit surveys – both before and after, and stay surveys which are focused to keep star employees. Regardless of the methodologies used to retain and sustain employees, each have advantages and disadvantages over the other.

Operational procedures should be evaluated with those who actually perform the work. When operational analysts talk only to managers, that analysis leaves critical elements out of the equation. That is, what challenges do each of your employee's experience when taking the steps to perform their work. Learning the steps employees actually do to complete tasks provide windows to discover hidden inefficiencies.

> "Technology may help structure the organization, but people run it"
> - Terrence Farrier

An example might be discovering why some areas of operations underperform, when typical analysis that does not include the actual job steps used to perform the job, reveal hidden actions. Studying those steps might also reveal repeated tasks performed in connective processes within the organization. When senior managers learn how much loss might be averted through the continuous improvement of efficient operations, they are most often surprised. So, for the sake of efficient and effective operations that decrease costs on the bottom line, removing possible biases from managers and evaluating the actual process from the viewpoint of the worker, is imperative.

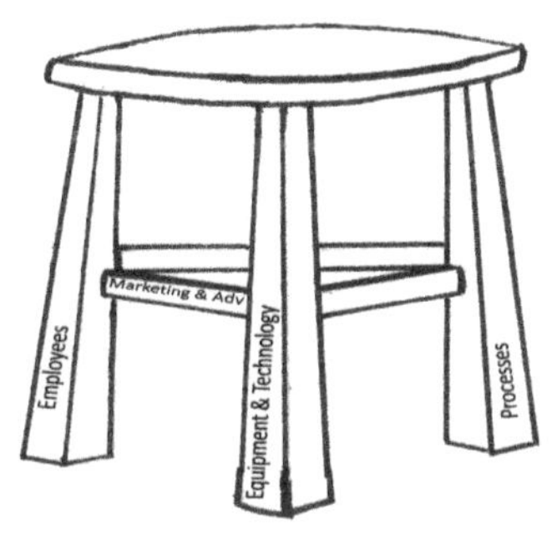

Chapter 5 – Marketing and Advertising

To some managers, marketing and advertising are straight forward business concepts which require little interpretation or discussion. According to Yohn (2019), those that believe that marketing and advertising do not play important pieces of the business decisions are mistaken. Others, who believe them important, sometimes overlook the connective tissue between operational processes, equipment capabilities, and employee capabilities that affect the focus of the marketing and advertising rung as depicted on the CCIM Three-Leg Stool. When senior and middle-managers really dig into the complexities of strategic business and organizational success, it becomes apparent improvements can and should be made, to improve this connectivity.

There are at least two primary parts of the marketing and advertising (M/A) co-dependent concept. First, advertising is a component of marketing, not vice versa. When people discuss M/A it is important to internalize that difference as they contemplate how to apply it. An example might help. A production business finds out through their purchasing department that they can purchase raw materials to manufacture products at a better price than usual. The seller of the raw material could only offer the special price for a short period, or maybe just that day. Once key decision makers within the production department find there exists excess capacity to store the purchase, if needed, they make the purchase and alert the marketing department. Then the marketing department can begin working on the advertisement of a special buy which allows a special promotion to the customer. The operations department is alerted that they will soon be receiving a glut of that certain product to produce and push the product out to the customer as the increased demands ramp up. Sounds simple so far…right? Maybe not!

The production department had been told to cut back spending by 10% last month and had reduced their full-time personnel to meet a corporate requirement. The glut of incoming product had to be bought Thursday of last week and the marketing department was told Friday which meant the advertising department was told on Monday morning and the operations department was told to prepare for the excess raw materials Monday afternoon. Unfortunately, the storage capacity to receive inventory for that same special purchase of the raw material is rented space that had capacity to hold only so much for so long. Ooops!

The company's purchasing process required same day sharing of information to include the production and marketing department. This accepted system allowed for continuity throughout the process to be discussed electronically, or if needed, a quick tactical video meeting. However, while purchasing the product at the special price, purchasing had not informed the production department.

This problem was exacerbated due to the production department's decrement of the 10% less production employees to do the job.

In this scenario, communications through company channels were not capitalized. Subsequently, purchasing had not followed policy concerning the processes section of the CCIM Three-Leg Stool. Therefore, management had to do two things to off-set the miss-step. They had to rent more storage and had to bring back employees to full-time status quickly. Associatively, this oversight resulted in a knee-jerk reaction to obtain greater profits and required emergency actions on the part of several connective departments. Thus, the extra profits were lost.

Also, reaction time to procure and produce product at the special price was lost. The seller of the discounted material only had a short time to offer the material at that price. So, they had to offer it at a first come-first buy situation. Therefore, this scenario could have given the competition time to buy the same raw materials to produce at lower prices. The gains that could have been captured ended up as resource losses and possibly losses associated with some customer base, and in the long-term possible losses in market-share.

Further, using the scenario above, if information got out to the customers that the company was about to have a major sale on a product line, they would expect it. However, the product did not get out at the leaked time and other competitive businesses that resell or budget to buy the product made their plans accordingly. What just happened? Marketing represents our ethics concerning everything we say publicly, everything we promise our employees, customers, and clients (both internally and externally). Marketing represents all that we do and directly affects how we are perceived, which impacts the brand of the company. In this case, the reliability and trust of the company just got a little injured. The examples of such could go on and on. If it is bad enough, it also means that marketing to customers may experience the need to provide damage control. So, how does a company guard against such contingencies? Two of the best ways is associated with excellent communication and the processes that are derived from policy and aligned procedures. [See Chap 4 & Chap 8].

Regardless of the business size, even if the company owns the largest market share, marketing and advertising are required. Now, more than ever the reach of customers through technology is easily and readily accessible. Also, if your company doesn't use those technologies, your competitors will! There are differences between the scope and wherewithal between types of businesses. Small businesses, big companies, and franchise startups must plan their marketing and advertising with different scales and scopes to gain momentum and keep it.

Small businesses often run out of resources before they gain traction in the marketplace. Most small businesses, who do not have deep pockets, need to concentrate on cash flow not profits, first. Why? Many small businesses think profits must come quickly to keep going. They concentrate on profits first. That is a mistake! Instead, small business should concentrate on cash flow which must keep coming in to allow more orders to produce more and more of what makes the small business profitable. Once a comfortable cash flow and savings are achieved, the concentration of profits can follow.

There is little room for error because there is not enough money in the small entrepreneur's pocket to adjust. if problems arise. Given this, the small business owner should review how he/she markets and advertises. This is especially true if the small business advertises that they will offer credit to customers or clients for their products or services. Further, he/she should learn who their customers are early, so marketing and advertising dollars are not wasted right from the very start of their opening the business. Due to that challenge alone, small businesses do not have the luxury to guess when marketing or advertising their offerings.

Larger businesses and franchise companies have some similarities with small business startups, but there are also some differences. Let us begin with the similarities. First, big companies who are in the business of new franchise starts should have enough back-up resources to engage in more risk. Despite rigorous analysis, some franchises do fail in some communities. Examples of franchise failure causes might be: An unannounced competitor moves in and drains profits from the new franchise market environment, natural or man-made disasters, and so on.

Next, once the budget for marketing and advertising is agreed upon, minimizing risk to fulfill those offerings to customers must be considered with secondary means of production, delivery, price, and customer experience should they be required. New franchise businesses which start by using the previous expertise of a small business manager must train the new small business franchisee to think more broadly in order to accommodate the strategic marketing and branding of the new franchise. That training is critical, and is sometimes overlooked by the new and inexperienced franchise owner. This happens more often than many might expect.

Small business owners with a certain expertise are often solicited to help new franchise starts due to their knowledge of a certain product or service that the franchisor wishes to capitalize on. No problem. However, when it comes to marketing and advertising, the small business owner might have only their past experience to build upon. In many instances I have seen the attempt of branding over-ridden in such situations. Attempting to diversify the intent of the franchise offering using small business marketing and advertising experience is risky without guidance utilizing a strategic viewpoint.

Imagine offering a specialized product or service and then advertising outside of that specialized area. The initial appeal for the customer, who thought the franchise was offering something new and possibly important to them, just went flat. At this point, the new franchise start-up just confused their fledgling customer base and broadened their competitive postures. They now offer what other competitors also offer. Accordingly, differentiation just died. Doing so could damage the branding of that franchise as a whole, not only locally, but also, if attempts continue - nationally.

For example, a start-up new franchise is offered to a community within a segmented market and focused their offerings to cater to families and business executives. The market and advertising supporting this segment touted that they provided healthy foods on a daily basis. The food could be obtained at the business location, or delivery options could be offered to either families or executives. However, the business owner began experiencing with left-over food, and decided to offer day old merchandise at a discount, at the same location. The management did not want to waste left-over food. Further, management decided as a matter of convenience, they would offer the left-over food at discounted prices at the same location. To make matters even worse, they offered the fresh daily food on one end of their display counter – and at the left-over food at the other end of the same counter. At that point, all of their previous marketing and advertising (M/A) focused toward branding as a food provided as fresh daily was destroyed.

Here is a second example of a M/A and branding failure. A new start-up franchise began M/A efforts that promised an authentic type of cuisine. Their product was exceptional, and their prices were competitive, if not slightly cheaper than their competitor's offerings within their same business or market segment.

> "Your personal brand serves as your best protection against business factors you can't control."
>
> - Dan Schawbel

However, the small business owner turned franchisee wasn't happy with the profits quickly enough. So, the new franchisee began to let the business owner operator to offer other products outside of their authentic cuisine and their marketing and advertising to slip toward those new offerings. The new franchisee and new business franchise owner exacerbated the mistake by beginning to advertise the new non-authentic offerings. The confused customers began to broaden their search for the new items and the competition for the business likewise broadened. Once again, the branding of the new franchise was destroyed.

In the above case, there are culpable problems attached to the small business-franchise-start-up. The first was financial. If, the new franchise start-up management had planned for unseen challenges, they could have had more finance reserves. They didn't. Because they felt insecure about the initial income levels, they decided to offer a broader and more socially familiar cuisine. Thus, second tier decisions (non-brand specific offerings) attached to the first mistake (not enough resources) culminated into an impulsive decision. Subsequently, the management failed to brand properly and focused on profits first – not cash flow.

Also, future attempts to brand become problematic. For instance, what happens to prospective customers once they perceive a dilution of the intended message? If that marketing and advertising leads to the confusion of prospective customers, the franchise may have to compete with all other competitors just to maintain solvent. Further, if that short-term franchise branding locks in, it will be duplicated in other franchise locations and environments unless the message is caught early enough. In short, those mistakes do not only fail to work, but it can often damage the branding and future marketing and advertising of the new franchise startup. The costs to re-align the branding, that was once not an issue because they were specialized in their offerings, can be worse and harder than starting up to begin with. Subsequently and unfortunately, that franchise start-up failed.

How much experimentation should be allowed between the small business owners compared to franchisee startups? After the proper analysis of the local or regional markets, for small and franchise businesses respectively, the products or services offered should fit the marketing provided to those markets. Also, the time, effort, and operational support must adjoin those efforts and abilities to maintain them. Remember, what cannot be supported in the long term, should not be started.

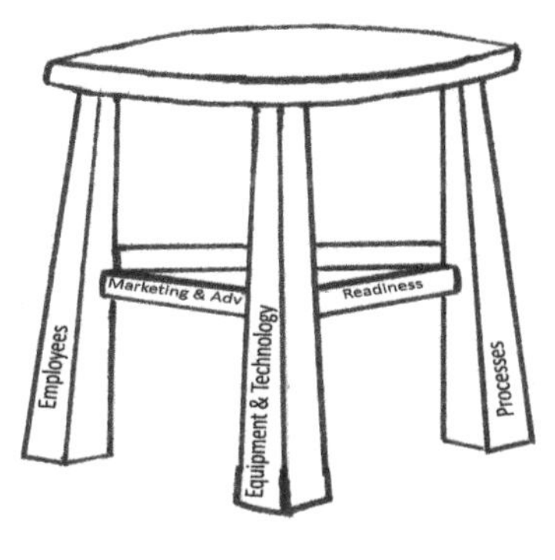

Chapter 6 – Readiness

All parts of a company will not be ready for change, nor will they accept change and improvement equally. When more than a cursory review of the company is completed, management will discover different parts of the company is more adaptive to change and continuous improvement than others. If the organization or company has been operating for some time, the divisions within them will have adopted strategies that work specifically for their divisions. This is a natural development. Accept that each internal culture, led by subordinate managers, may be different. However, as posited by Engle (2013) and Saberton (2018), these internal cultures (silos) may work well for their division, but that doesn't mean they work best for the company or organization. If those silos are not detected, resource losses will occur that may not be realized until severe damage occurs to the company.

Further, both Engle (2013) and Saberton (2018) stressed that silos can be symptoms of problems due to inadequate policies and procedures adopted and supported by management. Here are two primary things that contribute to the causation of silos. First, the fear of being outpaced by other departments (or sometimes individuals) as described in Hamel and Prahalad (1996), and being discovered as doing something a little outside the company policy.

Second, and supported by Ridge (2018), are how mistakes are handled by management. The second is conjoined to the first, because depending on the culture of the company, fear is the biggest culprit for both causations and how the company handles departmental and individual mistakes promotes the development of why and how silos develop. Exacerbating those two primary reasons for the development of independent silos is a new or novel product or service which may be a derivative of a product or service the company already owns, but others had not discovered yet, and using it only for the benefit of the independent division or unit only. Also coveting such discoveries can also lead to solicitations from other like recipients of such products or service that is not supported by the entire company. [See Chapter 4]. The discovery and how the management decides to adjudicate that discovery is the issue here, because the revelation of that new market segment could point to a new customer base that could lead to profits for the whole of the company. While creativity should be rewarded, the development of a new derivative product or service should be reviewed for inclusion and for the sake of the entire company.

So, how does company's management group meld creativity and curtail silo development? Senior management and company stakeholders should review their policies to see how they matriculate throughout their organizations, and how they are understood by each management level. Once the direction through policies are understood, change and continuous improvement initiatives should commence.

Also, done properly, your company will need both. Management must know which division can accept and will adapt to change and continuous improvement efforts more readily or may require training. Further, after senior managers learn which divisions are more or less adaptable, they should have a better understanding of how the entire enterprise can make sustainable adjustments that are supported through proper alignments.

Senior and middle-managers will always have detractors. Some business and operational units and individuals will resist change, even if the boss requires an overall cultural change for the total enterprise. According to Kotter (1996), some detractors will think change is too hard or takes too much effort and will subvert efforts to reduce responsibility. Unfortunately, sometimes management may have to extricate or move an employee to another position to enact change and continuous improvement policy or supporting operational efforts. Doing so might be uncomfortable, but also not doing it means ignoring the possibility of losing more employees later or worse the company. There are ways to lesson these impacts [See Chap 2 & Chap 8]. Further, updating or changing policy or procedures to improve operations is always a viable option, if it means the overall health of the organization might suffer otherwise.

Such change and continuous improvement efforts do not have to be negative and can rejuvenate the entire company. These types of thoughts are supported by Garry Ridge, President/CEO of WD-40, who refocused his entire organization to learn how to deal with mistakes (Ridge, 2018).

He believed learning from mistakes can be positive, if management allows it to be so. He focused on sharing the mistake and learning what caused it as something to be overcome, not just penalized, had a far more positive outcome for individuals, management, and the company. He believed that this formula can decrease fear and increase sharing. This belief is also shared by Gunn and Gullickson (2016), who posited that learning is important to companies and organizations. When a company doesn't review its policies and offerings it becomes too rigid and learning stops.

> "The longer you wait, the more entrenched the old system is."
> - Tony Hsieh

Organizational Structure/Hierarchical or Flattened?

Companies and organizations fall into general structures of either hierarchical or flattened. Hierarchical organizations are defined basically as having more layers of management. These layers are typically those that have senior to junior management relationships. Most management decisions come directly from the senior management and those junior to that position carry those decisions into their respective operations. Those organizations which are easily identifiable as hierarchical are the military, police departments, fire departments, and similar governmental entities.

Flattened organizations are described as those that have fewer management layers and management decisions are made across the organization. Typically, flattened organizations practice peer to peer management relationships and decisions are made likewise. As described by Craig (2018), companies who have adopted the flat organization include Zappos, Medium, and Buffer. These companies offer mixed reviews of their flattened structures. Their histories are revealing. Adopting flattened structures also required a different set of skills for leadership than had once been the hallmark for career progression.

Some of those problems stem from the acceptance of the flattened structural organization when the movement became vogue in the U.S. in the 1980s. It was nearly a craze for businesses to get it done. The concept sounded good, but it also depends on how the overall change was managed concerning re-process and re-procedural applications within the organization. Many of the functions that could be absorbed into upper or lower management were removed from middle-managers, as many of those middle-management positions became obsolete.

Therein lies the management challenge. The pressure to change the organization to a flattened set of managerial operations, was not always smooth. As described by Wulf (2012), there can be a catch for some of those flattened companies even decades later, not all companies followed through with flattening their organizations well. Admittedly, some of those job tasks should have been eliminated as they had become obsolete. Also, in the impulsive view of some managers, cutting out the middle-managers and reducing payroll was appealing.

The culture of flattening is still alive. That is not all bad. In some cases, it is very good. However, some job tasks, especially those that once seemed less efficient were summarily deleted without thorough analysis. According to Diamond (2019), quick decisions, with little oversight, may lead to confusion. So, adjusting to the flattened organization could cause some companies to lose continuities they once had with some customers and suppliers. Even today, some continuing propagations of lost, and outdated processes which do not align with other processes and procedural applications have become a burden to management when it comes to recapturing customer and supplier relationships. [See Chap 2].

Some companies still experience difficulties when tasks that need to be performed are lost in the fray of change. Especially if those tasks were to complete job responsibilities that were meant to matriculate into the servicing of customers or clients. Those companies still continue to repeat those discombobulated operational functions because they have been taught to. The junior managers continually repeat many of those discombobulated in-efficiencies which were passed to them through their mentors.

As surmised by Wulf (2012), sometimes pressure precluded the pragmatic review of the job functions that were once done well, have now faltered and are repeated each time the training does not consider both efficient and relational issues in tandem. Both are necessary, both are important, and more importantly today, it is critical. However, both those that flattened out their organizations well and those that didn't, have adopted a culture of saving money through cutting people first and not completely analyzing the steps that might be left out by deleting those positions. This is especially apparent when policy, processes, and procedures do not align. It is true!

When we first encountered situations that harken back to the flattening of organizations and their antecedent discombobulations, we thought we had to be mistaken. It turns out, we weren't. Unfortunately, some companies and organizations fail to review job descriptions with their associated and updated tasks and lose opportunities to restructure and re-align them so that efficient, relational, and fluid operations can continue. For some, repeating those discrepancies due to mis-alignments and left out procedures have become part of the culture. Those discrepancies cost the company much more resources than they realize. It happens in both civilian and governmental entities, and that problem is a real one.

It seems like a mixture of hierarchical and flat works best! According to Crush (2018), a leadership style that utilizes better communicative skills and reverse mentorship and cuts through most of the management discontinuities which can provide the best avenues for improved efficiencies and growth. Leaders using this type of management technique relate to project or divisional leads as individuals. [See Chap 7 & Chap 8]. As leaders re-evaluate and learn the new skills to lead people, and managers adjust to manage projects, the maintenance and CCIM sustainment are achievable through the support of employee creativity and ownership.

Can senior and middle-managers prepare your company or organization for such change? Yes. The readiness rung connected to the three legs of the Stool allows management to form a baseline of people, procedures, and process alignments in a phased continuous improvement plan. Senior leaders must evaluate where their company is currently, so the proper training can take place. Placing knowledge and importance on the whole of the organization, rather than the parts, must be the primary focus. The corporate policy is relevant from on-boarding employees [See Chap 2]. and continues to be relevant throughout the employee life-cycle. Training to meet policy and vision represents the whole of the organization. From the lens of readiness, it means that every layer of the organization will react in actionable, measurable, and continuous improvement ways to support sustainment.

Examples of failures in that area are Wells Fargo in 2016 and Starbucks in 2018. Wells Fargo incentivized their employees through sales, but management relied too heavily on sales figures which were based on how many on-line banking accounts they could open. Management's focus relied too heavily on sales incentives. Doing so led sales people and some employees to react by selling and supporting things that didn't exist. Wells Fargo nearly lost the company due to their employees opening up fake email accounts and fraudulently setting up online banking services and was fined $185 million for illegal banking practices and another $100 million from the Consumer Banking Protection Bureau.

Starbucks did not follow up on how the policies, processes, and procedures were understood and how their vision matriculated down to the store level. As reported by Samuelson (2018), the result was a store manager who allowed the ousting of two black customers who had spent time in the restaurant, but were also not purchasing foodstuffs or coffee at the time of their ousting on April 12, 2018. Spending time in the restaurant while awaiting the arrival of a business colleague, and without purchasing while in the restaurant, created confusion for the store manager and staff. Both companies were sued heavily for those mistakes. The CEO of Starbucks, Kevin Johnson sent a blast email to the media to apologize to its customers, and then had follow-up training for managers and employees so they understood the company policy better. In both companies, management had become complacent and had not reviewed, updated, and trained subordinate managers concerning their policies, processes, and procedures.

The lesson here is that management executives should review their incentive policies to see that they support the policies and vision of the company. Also, they should assure that the training is sufficient at all levels so that those policies and vision are understood and so such occurrences do not develop. From the readiness standpoint, it means learning who is capable to accept continuous improvement first, and then making sure each level of your management team reacts to situations that support the policy and vision of the company or organization.

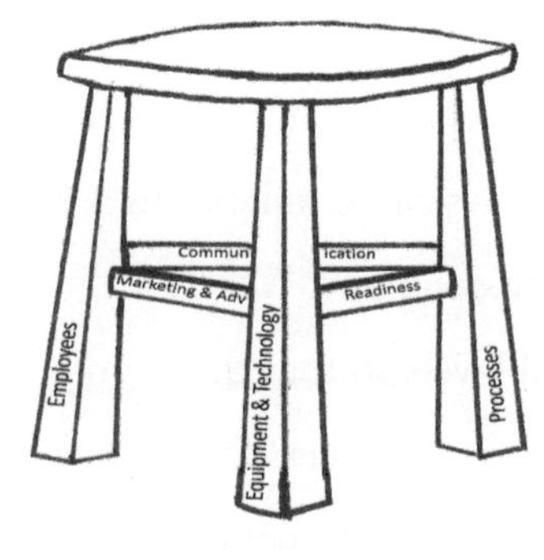

Chapter 7 – Communication

Improving a company's or organization's profits through policy updates and alignments, training, and job descriptions will not occur without reviewing and realigning communication practices. Communication remains as the underutilized profit center. Senior managers within companies and organizations understand it is important…but it is also underutilized (Heibutzki, 2018). So, if it is so important, why doesn't management pay more attention to it? After a career of working with companies and organizations, I can tell you from experience that communication is the main culprit which leads to losses and also that can be most easily trained to managers and controlled. It has been proven time after time, and it is why I consider it to be the most important rung on the CCIM Three-Leg Stool.

A key ingredient to the communications efficiency recipe is knowing the differences between how senior and middle-managers think. Such beliefs are supported by Verma (2016), who understood that the different thinking styles between the senior and subordinate managers can influence how the communications matriculate within the organization. These thinking styles, and in particular their differences, can affect how and what decisions result. Further, this point is amplified as the executive position increases.

The more senior the manager, the more communication training becomes critical, because senior managers typically impact the company or organization when communicating deeper and usually on more connective topics. As posited by Zerfass, et al. (2016), communications training for senior management is still needed to access and provide separate guidance to subordinate leaders. Our experience has shown that good communication between the senior managers and middle-manager decision-makers can add 3-6% profit to the operations segment on the bottom line.

The differences between these figures are of course connected to how well the company or organization communicates to individual managers and then to general employees to begin with. An alignment between policy, processes, and procedures connect directly to the efficiencies of the organization and the effectiveness of understanding between senior and middle managers and the workers who get the job done [See Chap 9].

From individual communication levels, senior managers might improve their own abilities to practice dialogue more often than focusing on meetings with discussion formats. There is a difference in the two, and it requires practice. Discussion usually requires one-sided wins while dialogue focuses on listening more closely to formulate win-win scenarios. Also, when dialogue is used at the management table between the senior and middle-management leaders, it helps the company divert challenges better.

As discussed by Turnage and Goodboy (2016), when using dialogue, managers can better focus on communications challenges. Further, as they practice the development of dialogue, it provides management with a venue for predicting problems and affords executives ways to support upper management better. Providing a venue to overcome communication challenges at those levels also helps the rank and file employee identify with a more concise understanding of the company, because the bulletins or stories they hear can be more focused and less derisive.

Clear understandings between management and employees provide continuity. According to Pendell (2018), merely 22% of workers compellingly agree their management has a decisive course for their company. Also, despite extensive communication plans, presentations and memos, few employees think their leaders know where their organization is headed. Further, just 15% of workers convincingly approve that their management creates enthusiasm about their futures. Therefore, properly conducted dialogue reduces challenges associated with mis-understandings whether real or surmised.

Complacent managers, who believe they communicate well enough already, may seem satisfied with the status quo. Believing so can be assumptive and dangerous to the overall health of the organization. Such dangers assert themselves in the forms of financial losses. [See Chap 6 - Wells Fargo and Starbucks]. However, if operational communication aligns with the process and procedural efforts, communication losses can decrease. Also, alignment may increase the corporate abilities to provide resources and budget outlays to correct mishaps should they occur. Communication inefficiencies burden budgets, and may hinder competitive focus which could slowly drain the organization's ability to forecast new products for analysis, challenge new and like businesses that compete with them, and complicates an organization's paths for long-term survival.

Informational Dissemination Tools

It is a natural occurrence for competitors to attempt to take market-share from your company or organization through making similar offerings with improved quality, price, or delivery options which may lead to better customer/client experiences. Improving communications throughout the company improves efficiencies and profits. Companies and organizations typically use a mixture of telephone, email, face-to-face, or company or social meetings to disseminate decisional information to subordinate managers and employees. Doctoral communications mixed-methods research involving 220 middle-managers (Farrier, 2017- See Table 3 & 4) indicated which company and organizational communications dissemination tools are most utilized, which work best, and where shortfalls existed.

Table 3

Comparison of Individual Delivery Tools/Most Utilized

IDT	*M*	*SD*	Df	*F* value	Pr > F
CSM	13.109091	12.24249			
Email	42.368182	23.38961			
F2F	31.313636	21.78762			
Telephone	13.209091	12.95521			
			3	136.2	< .0001

Note. $N = 220$, $p < 0.05$. IDT= information delivery tools; CSM = company and social meetings; F2F = Face-to-Face

These ratings reflect a per-cent of use for each IDT. The combined percentages had to total 100% for the individual combinations of IDT choice. The mean utilization scores for *use* are indicated from highest to lowest above in Table 3 with Email being the highest and Company Social Meetings being the lowest. However, differences exist in Table 4 below which displays what middle-manager participants believed to be the *most effective* of the four Information IDTs for the delivery of micro-operational guidance in businesses and organizations. The results indicated that the mean ratings for effectiveness indicated a significantly higher mean score for effectiveness occurs with face-to-face (F2F) use (M = 39.06) to make decisions while the lowest, telephone (tel) with (M = 10.36). Farrier's (2017) study, indicated while landline phone systems are dwindling in modern companies, they still hold a purpose. Interference experienced by cell phone users within built up areas still keep some land line phones useful.

However, landlines or cell phones are not the primary way that senior and middle-managers communicate to make decisions today, as they were only a short few years ago. Telephones, both land and cell phones, are used as the *third* method of dissemination of information providing decisional information, but they were also rated next to the *least* effective to deliver *micro-operational guidance.* Micro-operational guidance is guidance which is required (given the situation) to detail enough fidelity to meet the final tasks adequately.

Table 4

Comparison of Individual Delivery Tools/Most Effective

IDT	*M*	*SD*	Df	*F* value	Pr > *F*
CSM	15.159091	16.411577			
Email	35.418182	24.160945			
F2F	39.059091	24.550036			
Telephone	10.363636	11.02486			
			3	114.79	< .0001

Note. $N = 220, p < .05$.

The data projected that Farrier's (2017) study, suggested Face-to-face communication was rated the *second* most favored way for senior and middle-managers to disseminate decisional information, and it was also rated the *most* effective. This form of communication allows for questions and answers between the senior and middle-managers to improve clarity. Company or social meetings was rated as the *fourth* most widely used to disseminate decisional-information, however it was rated *third* on the effectiveness scale to communicate adequate micro-operational guidance information. Those social activities utilized a more relaxed atmosphere, but they also vary in informational agendas for each of the individual groups. As of 2017, email was the *primary* method for senior and middle-manager decision makers to communicate in companies and organizations, but it was also rated *second* on the effective scale.

Because managers utilize different technologies within companies and organizations, we must discuss other communications improvement considerations. The Community Toolbox (2015), posited that communication does not exist unless it is clear-cut, thorough, and recent. The degree of technical knowledge or operational steps may require more than being clear alone. An example might be:

Today is the 11th of May. John gets a directive from his senior manager which provided the following contexts: (1) Paint the house red. That is a clear directive communication, but it also lacks *thoroughness* and depending on the timing of that communication, it may, or may not, be *recent.* (2) Paint the house red by 2 o'clock today. That is a *clear* directive with a given timeframe and has increasing *thoroughness.* (3) Paint the house red by 2 o'clock next Wednesday.

Each of the examples above represents a progressively *clear* directive that infers *clarity*, increases *thoroughness*, and allows for planning and prioritization of jobs to be scheduled. Effective communication requires managers to disclose information to their subordinates that is understood and with enough depth to get the job done. Each company, or organization, will have job requirements that require more and some less guidance. Associatively, the right words have meaning and are understood and the wrong ones fall short of intent.

This truth was not lost on Faught (2016) who championed that the language, perceived intent, and lax attitudes in operational communications deter better performance. The faster a company must fulfill its customer or client requests, the more important communications become. Further, the more agile a company is, the more improving communications becomes important.

Things may change in the middle of the operation, so keeping competing priorities current will aid in the accomplishment of operational tasks and represent inputs to clear and effective communication. Also, as posited by Silic and Back (2016), who hypothesized it matters if the communication is delivered timely enough. Too often, middle-managers feel that decisional information they receive is not timely enough to accomplish their operational tasks.

Further, as posited by Farrier (2017), depending on the clarity of a message, its thoroughness, its timeliness, and the perception of that message by the receiver, *effective* communication may or may not occur.

A manufacturing example of clear and thorough information importance might be explained like this. A yarn fabric might require a new treatment or process in order to fulfill the customer's requirement. However, the yarn fabric treatment lies outside the normal specifications of the procedures which had become standing operational procedures for yarn products of similar types. If the differences in process is not communicated clearly, thoroughly, and is timely enough, disastrous problems could easily ensue. Mis-aligned processes can guide improper procedures of the yarn sample, either or both could cause a catastrophic failure of color, quality, or strength of the fabric. The entire batch of yarn may not be suitable for retail sales.

The frustration experienced by the senior and middle-level manager and the possible loss of the yarn sample is only part of the story. If the losses are great enough, stakeholders may want to know how the loss could have been avoided, or worse try to find fault in whoever was responsible. Additionally, hiding the process failure because proper communication (verbal or codified) does not occur might not improve communications and finally the managers and employees might not learn from the experience.

Multiple losses of this type usually do not go un-noticed. Also, repetition of losses due to mis-communication will lead to loss of trust between the original supplier of the components used to manufacture the product. Further, that loss of trust will exacerbate future buying decisions from customers who might purchase poor quality products, should those products pass quality inspection and get the information to the responsible plant that will treat, process, and perform quality assurance testing on the product. [See Farrier, (2017) table 5..below].

Table 5

Improvement of Individual Delivery Tools (IDT)

Priority	Timeliness	Personalized	No Issues	Confused	Follow-up	Thorough	Clarity
6	10	6	134	13	8	42	77
Total	Responses		296				
Original	Responses		220				
Mixed Rsp	Difference		76	0.35			

Note. N = 220

Farrier's (2017) study, indicated that *clarity* and *thoroughness* were listed as the *most important* to middle-managers. Of the two clarity was the most important (35%) and thoroughness (19.09%) following it as the *second most important* for middle-managers. These communication challenges were linked, as part of the challenge associated with clarity concerned thoroughness.

Also, those respondents who were confused, including those who couldn't be included in the completed study, because they didn't fill out each question, revealed that 35% of those respondents stated the clarity between senior managers and middle-managers could be improved. When clarity and the lack of thoroughness of information are weak, they affect every part of the organization to some degree. Further, the study indicated such inefficiencies exacerbate action, support non-action, and confuse recipients who must accomplish the task of work concerning how to react to the information disseminated.

Clarity and thoroughness have yet another component. The *form* of information is important to those who are tasked to complete the work. The forms of messages from the supervisors fall into two broad categories: *For your information* (FYI) and *for your action* (FYA). [See Table 6]. The initial form of communication denotes information that might be necessary should an immediate decision not need to be made, or might need to be made in the near future. The second informational form, FYA, however, may be understood as needing immediate action.

Also, the communication research Farrier (2017), indicated that 57.3% of middle-managers rated that mis-understanding and mis-information associated with the clarity of directions from their senior managers messages, actions not required versus actions required, was the *number one problem* between themselves and their bosses. So, how do the senior managers communicate information that is clear, thorough, and timely enough when utilizing the dissemination tools (telephone, email, face-to-face, or company or social meetings) and in the forms of information (FYI/FYA) matter? Or, more importantly why should it matter? Middle-managers rated the clarity of information disseminated from their senior managers, which caused mis-understanding and mis-information, between their actions between not required versus actions required as the *second* biggest challenge at 65.9%.

Table 6

Clarity, FYI and FYA, and the Decision-Making Processes

	Rated 1	Rated 2	Rated 3	Rated 4	Rated 5	Rated 6
Clarity	63	73	32	32	17	3
FYI/FYA	63/63	73/72	32/32	32/32	17/17	3-Mar
Tot/%	126/57.3	145/65.9	64/29.1	64/29.1	34/15.5	6/2.7
	Rat/Int	Rat/Int	Rat/Int	Rat/Int	Rat/Int	Rat/Int
DMP	53/47	51/49	59/41	58/42	55/45	58/42

Note. N = 220, FYI = For Your Information, FYA = For Your Action, Rat = Rational, Int = Intuitive, and DMP = Decision-making process

Further, there were significant correlations between FYI and FYA concerning the decision-making processes of the middle-managers. The middle-managers who also rated clarity and challenges with FYI/FYA as the first and second of the most challenges from senior managers, also had significant challenges associated with their own rational or irrational decisions based on that imprecise information.

Next, how do senior managers who communicate with middle-management pass information at the level of clarity, being thorough, and within enough time to be viable without micro-managing? There are three primary ways: (1) Use dialogue to ferret out mis-understandings, (2) allow the employees to own and exhibit personal pride associated with ownership to enhance the quality of your individual product or service, and (3) provide a feedback channel to the creators of those ideas, which can cycle back to the original creators, so that they know their efforts were acknowledged whether they are adopted or not.

Using dialogue so that all middle-managers can be heard and utilize their talents in a cross-leveled project atmosphere heighten understanding, acceptability, and trustworthiness. When understanding between peer middle-manager groups begin to gel, they also begin to focus on how to make their co-dependent operations work together better. Bonds and pride of ownership begin to form and after some time, trust. [See Chap 2/Cultures].

Middle-managers can learn from bad decisions as well as good, if they know why something did not work or if it worked well. Ridge (2018), believed that attempts and failures are part of learning and should be part of middle-manager training. Understanding the why allows them to adjust from a historical concept, but also be aware that if something did not work, it doesn't mean the idea or concept was bad, but it may not be the right time to implement it. Thus, either way, learning occurs.

Tying the Communication Profit, Efficiency, and Effectiveness Center Knot

Studies have confirmed that companies should make communication their 1st Tier in operational policy. When managers think about it, not much happens without communication first. Further, as championed by The Community Tool Box (2015), not much happens well in operational exchanges unless the transfer of communication is comprehended and made actionable. These alignments to support organizations are critical to success, because the inculcation of these business and organizational tie-ins reduce losses for the company.

Learning where losses occur through job description obsolescence and actual tasks performed is one thing, matching those tasks to the equipment and technologies make those operations efficient, then tying those processes into how those operational communications matriculate throughout your organization and is understood by the managers and employees lead to effective systems. To find out how those communications move through your company and become ingrained into your culture through processes, it is important that both senior and middle-managers know which information delivery tools are used most often, by who, and what challenges each of those tools present to each part of your organization.

Note, the communication preferences, utilizing studies similar to those found in [See Tables 3, 4, 5, and 6] for your company or organization. Then learn why those preferences exist in your organization. Next, streamline them so understanding and action takes place not only through administrative codification, but it can also become part of the employee culture when your managers leave the room. Understanding the complete story will help senior and middle-managers decide what training the senior and middle-manager groups need and whether that training should be internal or external. In short, learn why preferences are what they are. Whether communications are codified into centralized policy with decentralized applications, or updated job descriptions that produce alignments with equipment and technologies, to the processes and procedures that provide efficiencies and customer satisfaction those should matriculate throughout the organization so that co-dependent systems can be supported. Once communications efforts align with systems management, the ease of adjusting from an updated and known organizational baseline can be understood throughout the organization, and the impact can be both measurable and undeniable.

So, how do the senior and middle-management get their company or organization there? The answer is by removing as many emotional judgements from the communications analysis as they can. Be sure there is little impact from outlying inputs to communication which can result in poor middle-manager's decision-making. Farrier's (2017) study, indicated how those communications are understood and are made actionable within your organization so that they come to life when the senior manager's communication is compared to the middle-managers understanding of those communications.

Then senior management can analyze how middle-manager's like, or dislike how the senior managers communicate with them. At that point stakeholders will understand how the matriculation of communication truly works within their organizations and can find ways to improve them.

Also, management and stakeholders must be strong enough, and to be honest with themselves, once the analysis is completed. Not everyone will accept that a change in communication is necessary to obtain better process and customer satisfaction. However, an honest assessment, which is the precursor to finding out how much your organization's communication require updating can work, and can support continuous improvements so that the organization can remain strategically competitive. It is a critical step in improving any company or organization's future. The tests to find out where your organization currently sits along the communicative timeline, are both psychological and pragmatic. Although the most senior manager needs to set the pace and tone, all employees must understand and feel integrated. [See Chap 10/Change Management].

Communications improvement can actualize the knowledge and skills of your employees so that management can enhance processes alignment and efficiencies to obtain maximum quality of your product or service. Lean, Lean Six Sigma, and Operations Research Systems Analysis (ORSA-Army), International Organization for Standardization (ISO), etc., processes allow some of these identifications to occur. However, none of them alone create the understanding of the needs of the customer and the strategic efforts required to attain and sustain those essential processes for and within the company or organization. They each require parity with the communication analysis as described in [See Tables 3, 4, 5, and 6] and the co-dependent preceding chapters. Both senior and middle-managers must analyze the connections between policies, processes, and procedures within and across your company to achieve the bench-marks required to achieve continuous improvement.

Is there a caveat? Yes. For the company that is trying to attract new business is it always practical to be overly cautious concerning losses in the beginning? No. If a company stretches its funding to attract new customers, and challenges its internal systems to break the mold in a market segment to get the new customer, it is not always bad. Competitive posturing may require it. The key concept and concern for stakeholders of the company is this - before management makes that investment for that new customer, make sure the company policy, processes, and procedures are in place so that there exists a sustainable plan to support that concept. [See Chap 3]. Otherwise, senior managers should address how and when the company will not or will no longer offer it.

As espoused by Hamel and Prahalahad (1996), do not set yourself up for losing money by setting a precedence the company cannot support. Why? Other customers may compare themselves and want preferential treatment when your company decides to support that precedence. Note that setting a precedence can be impractical and dangerous. If your company cannot fund or maintain the on-boarding of the new customer, either specialize your product or service to meet the needs of that new customer or client, or divest some of your business portfolio and let the satellite operation fill the gap. This is where operational policy and processes become important.

Further, operational processes fall within the guidelines of your organizational policies so that systemic and supporting elements congeal. According to Gandhi (2018), company and organizational policies project the general direction for the corporate plan and hopes for a sustained future. Managers and team leaders put the policies in action. However, how middle-managers and team leaders read, interpret, and apply those polices can differ. Subsequently, what realities are experienced by workers and eventually customers and clients can be different due to those non-parallel understandings and later actions. [See Chap 6/Wells Fargo/Starbucks]. Managers and leaders must understand how these policies and subsequent actions are to be brought to align and project the overall goals of the company or corporation for their employees.

Although not the overall focus of this book, while senior and middle-managers endeavor to improve communication skills between them, it is important to remember how the employees understand these differing levels of managerial direction as they culminate into actionable results for the organization. This is especially true if employees are made up of different cultures or communications must cross into different units of the company. This is a valid point, because many employees will communicate differently depending on their cultures and their divisional silos (units) within the company. According to Early (2017), when a company is made up of workers that are from more than two differing cultures, it is imperative that the communication efforts consider those differences and unite efforts that support conversation.

Further, according to Colrus (2019), cross level communication, the communication across different divisions in the business and the different levels of responsibilities, can be significant. The size of the business will impact this of course, but it can also mean that sometimes managers forget it when ramping up or down operations occur in their areas of responsibilities. Ineffective communications lead to reduction of morale, employee losses, inadequate productivity, and which subsequently can affect profits. That is why the communication rung is the champion of the rungs that support the legs and the seat on the CCIM Three-Leg Stool.

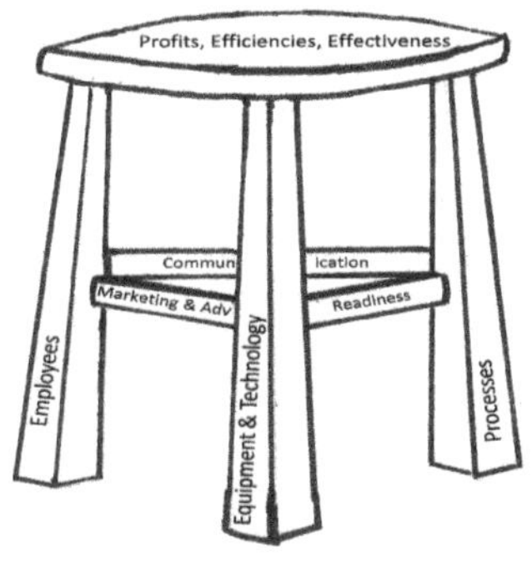

Chapter 8 – The Seat (profits, efficiency, effectiveness)

All three legs of CCIM Stool must support the seat to achieve successes. Senior managers should continually evaluate the legs, so that the seat does not become off-balance resulting in operational and strategic loses. Each functional business, organization, or governmental entity has its own individual requirements so that they remain stable and efficient, right? Yes, and no. Systems management allows both senior and middle-managers to cut across functional divisions to achieve a sustained set of operations; that benefit the longevity of their organizations.

So, how do senior managers, stakeholders, and middle-managers deal with the myriad of informational inputs from both the internal and external environments? The secret is learning to break down each function or operation into its finite parts, then comparing them to the rest. When completed correctly, those comparisons lead to solid policy effectiveness that reaches across the entire organizational enterprise.

If your organization isn't doing this now, it should be. Ignoring your ability to enact continuous improvement; or remaining complacent, and may allow your competitors to easily take the lead and stay ahead. This leads me to discuss how company and organizational change management is not only necessary, but also crucial. However, how senior and middle-managers decide to change and improve their organizations or their corporations, matter. Those efforts can be mis-guided, and at most harmful.

I have witnessed two primary outcomes when companies or organizations make changes to enhance profits. The first; is dismissing people to decrease payroll, and the second is re-organization.

The easiest and least involved for change to cut costs for most managers involves the termination of employees. Usually, those employees terminated are those who have earned longevity with the company and are paid the most, or cannot learn technology quickly enough to meet competitive challenges. Sometimes terminating long-time employees or terminating due to re-organizations can be necessary, but it can often also depend on how management implements those directives so they are more thoughtful, more ethical, and make more business sense. So, what must managers do when their senior manager says cut employee costs?

As pressured management wrestles with the consideration of employee loyalty, other and possible longer-term effects on the company might become significant. How will those workers who are still employed see the termination, and the impact costs to train a new employee to the company climate. There may be other, and better options. [See Chap 4].

As an example, moving the employee to another needed position that benefits the organization and the employee, may be the better alternative. Even if the pay remains the same or the technological requirements are less, a known vacancy is filled and the employee job description analysis and retaining the long-term employee who is already updated and vetted [See Chap 2] into the culture and company climate. At this point, each ethical behavior might be noted by others, including perspective job seekers. Chances are likely, current and prospective employees might now see the move as more moral and ethical.

Also, management can capitalize on the training dollars previously spent associated to obtain and train the soon to be transferred employee, when comparing the costs of hiring a new employee. Further, as supported by Accurate Personnel Services (2019), managers can sometimes miss the mark when considering the cost associated and the time spent on trainers, other employees helping to train the new employee, and how long it takes to inculcate a new employee to the cultural organizational fold. [See Chap 3]. Those training dollar costs to indoctrinate the new employee to the company culture; are sometimes overlooked.

Pragmatically, senior and middle-managers should know that the ultimate quality, least cost, and quickest time cycles can only be attained through the elimination of waste. Achieving those standards; are impractical without both upper and middle-manager involvement associated with end-to-end process alignments. As internal alignments occur, the management thoughts should begin to extrapolate outside of their internal systems. Also, there are co-ordinations that may require reaching into external efficiencies to support the customer base, and expanding them.

Management and Employee Relationships

Fred, a mid-level supervisor, had been working for WXN technologies for years. He remembered several occasions that involved both workers and management, and he was remembering and sharing this story. It was easy for him to tell about worker stories, because he was an immediate supervisor of a manufacturing group. He went on to explain that he seldom saw upper management; on the manufacturing floor.

Fred began by telling an interesting story about Fannie R., who came to work in his plant. She had only been working with Fred six months, was a divorced mother of two, and had brought with her backgrounds in manufacturing from other plants. She worked in the corner of the plant, so he did not go to see her as often as his other 16 workers.

Fannie was a hard worker, and she always arrived early to get started and set up her machinery. So, it was no surprise that her production and quality numbers were always higher than the rest of his crew. One morning, when the workers were on a break, Fred also found himself caught up on his production status paperwork. So, he took another tour of the manufacturing floor. Somehow, he ended up in Fannie's corner.

For the first time, he noticed an odd addition to Fannie's work area. She had taped assembly parts hanging from a rope, directly from the ceiling. Also, she had attached a not so artistic one string pulley to it. Further observation revealed the rope supported taped parts in groups of five, which could be pulled down with a simple flick of a wrist. Immediately, Fred's reaction was the concern about a safety violation. However, he surmised the additional hardware represented no danger, as the parts were light and everyone on the floor was required to wear OSHA compliant grade helmets, steel toed work boots, and goggles.

However, Fred's curiosity was getting the best of him. Fred decided to wait at Fannie's work station; to discuss this oddity. Returning from break and noticeably a little un-nerved, Fannie asked Fred what was up? Fred merely pointed at the rope and tape contraption. Fannie replied, it helps me do my job better. Fred asked her to explain. She reviewed he work operations with him. She stated there was no more room to stage these parts on her assembly and press machine work platform. Given that situation, she would have been forced to wait for the quality control (QC) bin to reach her for the parts, to complete her assembly task.

Fred already knew her workmanship, from assembly through quality, was above everyone else's on the floor. So, bypassing a procedure wasn't an immediate issue. However, her explanation truly didn't explain how the parts ended up on the rope, tape, and pulley system. Fred wondered why waiting on the QC department bin to reach her assembly area; had not affected the other assembly workers. So, he asked how she got the parts more quickly; than her other co-workers? Fannie explained; that ever since the smelter and press were moved to the other side of the plant, QC's normal time to check for product quality had been lengthened, because the QC mobile operations station was also moved to one corner of the plant with the smelter and final press production. That meant getting the parts back to the assembly side of the building; took longer. However, the parts she retrieved, as she set her machine up each day, had already been through QC, as they had been before the smelter and final press production move. She could pick them up on her way to her station; as she returned from the break area. Additionally, she might pick up a few on her way to and from the bathroom. So, she had picked up a few parts on each occasion and hung them for easy retrieval, so she didn't have to wait.

At first, Fred was concerned about how Fannie's apparent short-cut might get both he and her into trouble, but he was also surprised by Fannie's ingenuity and perseverance. Fannie noticed the concerned look on Fred's face, and asked him if she should stop. Fred said no; not yet. Fred walked the route Fannie had taken through the plant, and passed the breakroom and bathroom. He noticed the availability of the parts, which had already passed the QC evaluation, near her daily pathways.

Fred knew the plant had been reorganized nine months earlier, and many machines were relocated including the smelter and final press areas. So, he asked the plant engineer to show him the movement blueprint. After talking to the plant engineer, Fred revealed that Fannie had compensated for a gap in the oversight of procedures, and had developed her own solution.

Fred took the situation to his boss, the production VP, and explained the oversight. After a short tour, and a review of the production figures compared to those of nine months earlier, the production VP was quite happy to agree with Fannie and subsequently Fred's surmise. An analysis was in order. Further examination revealed that it was not cost effective to move the smelter and final press areas again, due to the footprint of the assembly floor. So, the operational layout could not be changed.

Also, the analysis proved that to get more room on the floor would mean the elimination of two of the 16 assembly machines from Fred's area. Knowing how Fannie's solution had improved her work output, Fred was undeterred. So, a more efficient pulley device was devised to hang above the assembly machines, which took no more floor space and was similar in comparison to Fannie's original solution. Additionally, a part-time QC parts runner was hired to get the freshly inspected parts; from the smelter and final press areas, to the assembly floor. This eliminated the time Fannie used to take to retrieve the parts, on her own. More importantly, Fannie's idea changed the way 16 other assembly workers retrieved their parts!

Within two months, Fred's assembly area increased their weekly production by 7% and resulted in a 2% increase in quality product post assembly. That 7%, increase in production and 2% increase in quality product were spread over 16 machines which added a significant improvement to production and quality over the next year for the entire assembly floor. The production VP offered Fred a raise for finding out about the process oversight. Instead, Fred told the production VP that it was Fannie who deserved the praise. Any praise should go to her.

> "When people are financially invested, they want a return. When people are emotionally invested, they want to contribute."
>
> \- Simon Sinek

Looking back, that extra walk Fred took toward Fannie's workstation paid off. Before then, the plant did not have an idea or better solutions box. Fred and Fannie changed that. The production

VP got Fannie a very nice bonus check, and she was quite happy. Fannie's name and picture were then posted all over the plant, and WXN's internal plant flyer depicted her photo, and a special recognition lunch was held in her honor.

Fred was proud of Fannie, and each time Fannie was praised, it reflected on his assembly group. It didn't stop there. The other workers on the assembly group were told by Fannie how Fred had told the production VP about her solution. Fred's integrity had earned him respect on his floor, and was noticed by other executives. They now knew Fred was more than a mid-level manager. Fred now serves as the assistant to the plant manager, and as lead for the continuous improvement division.

While this business relationship game is portrayed in a manufacturing setting, these operational and relational settings could easily be incorporated universally, to fit most business and organizational situations. Managers who set aside the time to review their policies, processes, and procedures and focus on creative solutions may sometimes find un-polished gems in their area of responsibilities.

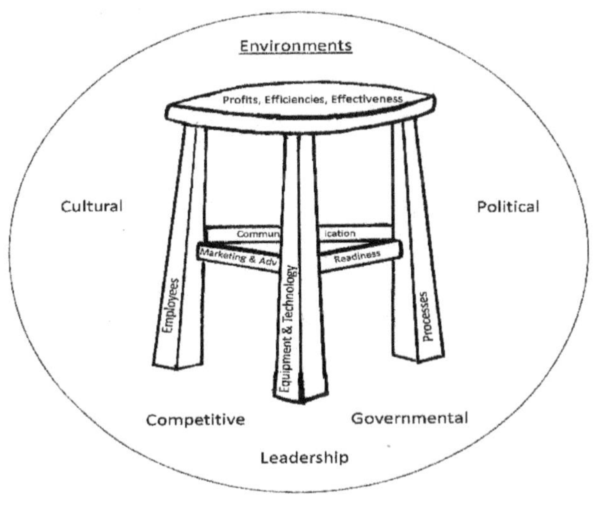

Chapter 9 – The Environments

Companies and organizations don't operate in a vacuum. Things change. In fact, things change so rapidly that companies and organizations can have a real challenge to keep up. Even worse is the glut of information with which leaders have to keep abreast with to lead well. That is the secondary reason this book was written. Through the parsing of successful operational segments, this book can help senior managers, middle-managers, and government/ military leaders take that glut of information, and parse it into the CCIM Three-Leg Stool environment. It helps it all make sense. As new information continues to impact the corporate decision making, the enticement to surrender to some of it will change too. However, when introduced to the CCIM Three-Leg Stool it helps to make it manageable, and better understood. That information has a place to reside, so that it is easier to digest, and can be incorporated into the environments in which differing organizations inhabit.

Those environments include the cultural, competitive, governmental, political, and the leadership environments. The CCIM Three-Leg Stool sits firmly in the middle in each, and in all, of these. While managers have little, if any, control over outside environments, how they help their companies react to changes of those outside environments can be orchestrated. Also, once the organizational challenges are met, the senior managers must always keep in mind how the strategic environment impacts their next move.

It may be useful to use another manufacturing example. Watoski Parts Operations (WPO) makes widgits for an automotive assembly plant. Then along comes a new company, Balvet Assembly and Tortion (BAT), who doesn't make widgits for the automotive assembly plant, but also uses the same raw material supplier as WPO. The plant that provides the raw material for the widgets that WPO builds, cannot supply both efficiently. If the contract is written well, WPO should still be OK, because they would have the first rights to a specified amount of raw materials that allow them to produce the widgets. Business for WPO can continue with little risk, because this arrangement allows WPO to stock and continue to warehouse, sell, and distribute inventory.

However, it is up to the supplier to keep those contractual obligations. During further investigation of the contract, the supplier noted that a contingency clause which insured for business necessity should the business environment change, could allow the supplier to over-ride the understood relationship with WPO concerning the first rights of raw materials. This meant that should BAT offer more dollars than WPO for the contracted raw materials, it may be a challenge.

Depending on how the contract was written (first rights having priority over the supplier business necessity-even during environmental change – or similar), WPO may be in jeopardy based on the business necessity of the supplier. Business necessity, when they are due to environmental changes, may not be covered in the contract - or at least well. In this case, and at minimum, the competitive market changed when BAT entered the stage. Even though BAT was not making the same product as WPO, they used the same raw materials. Managing contracts and providing oversight for changes to contracting agreements might help to minimize business risks. In this case, the job descriptions for WPO contract writers didn't change, but their competitive environment did. [See Chap 2].

Governmental

Governments also have cycles. Local impacts from political and governmental agendas may be different, from those with a national scope. Therefore, states and communities that differ in their views of governmental issues could impact your business. Taxation, health coverage, worker rights, and the support, or the withholding of support, of large versus small businesses from governmental resources can mean a lot to your organization and its plans. Even if your company or organization must follow large business regulations, your small business suppliers may not – and vice versa. Given these examples, governmental challenges to businesses might swing to the advantage of your company's competitors, or it may not.

Also, suppliers may have to charge more for raw materials or products due to impacts from import and export taxes. Such challenges might require a company or organization to change from one location to another state, or even another country, including some of their branch operations. Additionally, challenges in areas involving possible conflicts of governmental involvement affecting costs, might require a cursory review. For instance, a shrewd and pragmatic review of your company, which compares and contrasts your company with other like businesses, who might not allow employees to enjoy a fair wage, or do not support their communities, may be part of your business plan, because the government may decide to enact adjustments.

Further, governments can involve themselves using economic tools under the banners of free markets, social programs, or a mixed version of all of them. As championed by Alfredo (2017), who summarized the significance of how a business might develop through an understanding of how the government intervenes, if the government deems a business out of conformity with economic standards within these frameworks, they can reduce support programs previously enjoyed by the firm or organizational group. For instance, and according to Jensen (2017), some of the regulations that are upheld through government regulations which might increase business costs for companies that that have over 50 employees are the Family and Medical Leave Act (FMLA) and the Affordable Care Act (ACA) among others. Another example, KMJ23 (2016) cites that government and business regulatory challenges might deny the merger of companies to support anti-trust law legislation. This could affect the attainment of small business loans, should governments influence the regulation of monetary systems. Further, country or regional exchange rates might impact businesses, when large purchases are made and are represented by loaner debt.

Understanding how these challenges can affect your business and attracting and retaining employees with the skill sets to mitigate them is strategic, and provides for some risk protection.

Governmental influence can reach deep into the business operations should oversight include the stipulation of break and meal-time periods, legislation that affects the holidays and family leave (paternal/maternal), tax breaks or denial of tax breaks. From these economic and regulatory structures, the government can enact legal and binding policy to imply and enforce the necessity of business governance which result in increased costs. Also, governments could change their requirements and business protocols through direct business regulation, which can affect both business costs and operations. As an example, the U.S. Securities and Exchange Commission announced the requirement for the Sarbanes-Oxley compliance regulations of 2002. These requirements as explained by DefendX Software (2018), were meant to protect the public and the businesses, but they also require a more pragmatic accounting of business operations. These regulatory requirements have a direct cost which affect the business bottom line.

Further, as discussed by Corr (2018), governmental instability in international environments, can also affect business operations. Hostile overthrows of governments will directly impact businesses that operate within them. Examples of businesses within these environments are many, including: those which are affected by the Israeli and the Palestinian conflicts, Syrian disturbances, relationships between Iran and the U.S., China and the U.S., and so on. There are analysis tools that can help to mitigate risk for businesses that operate internationally. For instance, the political, economic, social, and technological (PEST) analysis gives businesses a good indicator of the elements that can impact the company or organization. Further, a deeper analysis can be used called PEST(LE) which also includes the legal and environmental elements of the analysis.

Political

It is important how your company interfaces with those who you do business with, from both the local and international standpoint. When political agendas impact your customers, suppliers [to include methods of distribution and supply management operations], and add any operational constraints to their focus as to how they will do business with your organization, your costs might also change. As an example, new political administrations restructure corporate regulations and tax laws with some regularity. At the time of this writing, another indicator for interface re-adjustment might be, according to Tatum (2019), the Trump administration announced an executive order requiring many employer-based group health plans and health insurance providers to divulge their prices and cost-sharing data to participant groups. This rule is to take effect in January 2021 and with the Department of Health and Human Services oversight.

Obviously, initial costs will at least increase for these entities. Senior leaders within health provider corporations, who work with those federal agencies, must see that adapting to those fluid situations remain amenable, even while they are pursuing opportunities as they become detectible elsewhere. Further, businesses that must connect and support such changes, might have to adapt to those changes quickly, and certainly before their competitors who may adjust to work with them.

These political changes could affect business organizations and could introduce a risk factor, that could cause your business to suffer a loss. Companies and organizations must plan for the variability of government policy and regulations and evaluate the platforms of politician's when they run for local, state, and national elections. Some, or many, of your customers may also fall into categories which may also be impacted by political agendas. Also, politicians have an obligation to serve their constituents. If their constituency is entrenched in a social imbalance such as: race, sex, wage differentials, housing, economics, infrastructure or township rebuild, and so on – your company needs to be aware of it. Examples might be, how political parties view ageism, health issues, poverty, or crime issues, Opinion Front (2019). The blurring of political parties makes it more important to know what your customers think, even if your company, as a whole, feels differently.

> "It's never paid to bet against America.
> We come through things, but its not always a smooth ride."
> - Warren Buffett

Also, politicians pay attention to the work environments when they are associated to constituents, and the possibilities of government business interventions, in their areas of concern. As stipulated by Harter, Agrawal, and Sorenson (2014), politicians also know that nations which have larger percentages of unhappy workers could also mean larger unemployment and underemployment rates. Therefore, a new political administration and changes in political policies can have severe impacts on international markets, employment and unemployment direction, employee attitudes, and buyer confidence to mention a few challenges.

Economic

The political environment in a country can affect its economic environment. The economic environment, in turn, affects the performance of a business organization. As posited by Harter, Agrawal, et al. (2014), leaders, politicians, and policymakers should work with companies and organizations to expand prospects for job growth. Positive economic inputs, both local and national, matter. Companies and organizations should identify and know the significance of employing and developing exceptional management to support worker engagement and throughput, which may affect their community, state, or nation's overall economy. [See Chap 5].

Leadership along these lines have implications for factors such as taxes and government spending. For instance, a higher level of local, state, and national government spending tends to stimulate the economy. Politicians might try to focus on those economies, where government spending budgets benefit their constituents. The more funds channeled into their constituent pool, the better that parsed constituency improves constituency wealth (this of course is impacted by the level of office).

Unemployment and worker disengagement [See Chap 2] also affects the macro-economy. Disengaged workers are not motivated employees, and do not add to economic stability. As espoused by Harter, Agrawal, et al. (2014), nations exhibiting the largest numbers of vigorously dis-engaged workers also had twice the number of people unemployed compared to employed and engaged workers. Expectedly, the number of vigorously disengaged workers fell from 14% to 8% when unemployment decreased. Reading the macro-economy with this lens, provides fidelity. If someone is unemployed, they can't be an engaged worker. So, more information may be necessary to support informed decisions.

Also, Harter, Agrawal, et al. (2014) denoted that when it comes to workers being disengaged, there are differences between employed, not employed, and underemployed. In nations with the largest percentage of vigorously disengaged employees, 22% were under-employed. This means, they were unemployed or employed some of the time, but they were also looking for full-time employment. This compares to 16% where the smallest number of dis-engaged employees were also unemployed or partially employed. This challenge exists across regions and nations, globally. Further, the higher level of vigorously dis-engaged workers a company has, the less your company will experience job creation and active growth.

Cultural

Your business or organization operates within a cultural environment, which can also impact your profits. Many of your business decisions, from whom your company hires to where your company decides to locate offices, affect the social and cultural environment in which they operate. How your company communicates their organizational values matter, in all of them. As an example, and decried by Dvorak and Nelson (2016), only 27% of today's U.S. workforce believes strongly in the organizational values projected by their companies. Your organization may encounter even more potential cultural and social risks, if your company expands into other countries. Knowing the cultural risks in advance, can help your corporation alleviate problems so that your business can continue to function smoothly with less interference or complications.

Also, your business or organizational location, also matters. According to Ray (2017), the historical legacy of a community will impact how your business is viewed and accepted by the local inhabitants. Companies can't change history, pro or con. However, management can help to show your customers or clients how they will improve the past, through the lens of historical contexts. If localized customers/clients have experienced organizations that have damaged their trust, time is not on your side. The sooner your company can overcome the fears of the past, the better. Ignoring local customs can fuel unfortunate media reports and poor community relationships, which in turn can lessen profits.

Further, the more social platforms are used within these communities, the more quickly the customers or clients can speed to share the news of a satiated or dis-satisfied experience with your company. [See Chap 5]. Also, social platform connections allow your competitors to know the breadth of your operations, and likewise the depth of any dis-satisfaction of your company. Competitors can quickly capitalize on damaging information, and attempt to convince socially connected customer bases that they can better serve them in the marketplace.

Competitive

Competitive business environments are as multiplicative as there are businesses that support them. Any successful business, will sooner than later have competition. The more marketplace your organization owns, the bigger target for your competitors. Thinking your company has a niche that has few competitors, is dangerous. Also, as discussed by Bergen and Peteraf (2002), it is important to analyze competitors from a broad perspective initially, so that business management planners do not overlook possible challengers, and risk a myopic approach to competitive analysis. Further, Info Entrepreneurs (2009), reflected that you can be sure that if more profits are to be made in your market segment, someone will be trying to figure out how to use your organization's weaknesses, that might spell profits for them. Your competitors will eventually attempt to emulate your product or service, or improve upon either of them.

A business that produces or provides services that are basically the same can, and usually do, have different cultures and attitudinal competitive environments. The cultures and attitudes attached to geographical, political, or loyalties can be different. This is true, whether your business is in a small business market segment or an international one. For instance, the same business with the same product or service located across town can have different environments. Their local customers may have different income levels, different political views, different overall ethnic characteristics, and so on. Therefore, they will purchase different things, purchase at different times, or purchase for different reasons.

Business stakeholders and executives are using more and more time attempting to figure out how to keep their current customer base and expand their market share. Most often, they focus to find out how to cost-effectively reach new customers and opportunities for growth. Also, as surmised by Kramer (2019), more and more companies are beginning to realize they cannot compete, solely on price.

Price strategies alone is becoming a no-win scenario, because sooner than later, even if your company has the opportunity to buy vast quantities to achieve the lower price, the cost-benefit of the supplier will reach parity. This is known as the *price-spiral.* Once the purchase prices from the supplier reach the point of diminishing returns, the purchasing company or organization must adjust to new tactics to keep their market segments.

Market segments exist because groups of customers have become familiar with expectations and experiences associated with their given market characteristics. When prices look too similar to their competitor's, businesses must change the structure or offerings to provide a different product or service. Good examples in the retail industry might be the change from original retail stores aspects toward the warehouse offerings and prices associated with opportunities within Sam's Clubs, Costco, and so on. Sam Walton opened the first Sam's Club on April 7, 1983 and Jeffrey Brotman and James Sinegal opened the first Costco later than same year. So, it has been some time since pricing strategies alone occupy the purchasing customer's viewpoint. Customers are looking for more opportunities to satiate themselves over price. Companies and corporations can bet the price spiral, and the difficulties that exacerbate the purchase of products at ever lower prices, is knocking at their doors.

Subsequently, a proactive and ongoing research of your competition to keep ahead and move forward of marketplace adversaries is required. Businesses that begin to see their markets shrink, may have already waited too long. That doesn't mean give up. However, it does mean examining what weaknesses exist in your organization, so that your competition does not use them to their advantage.

According to Kenton (2019), relationship management will remain a better avenue to identify new sales opportunities. We believe relationship management will increase in importance to offset price competition and a good way to correct and out-pace your competition. Albeit, whether your company stakeholders and or management group choses to compete by price point, on-time deliveries, quality, the communications between your company and your customers, or efficiencies in your operations, your company should not sit by and watch as they prosper and you close your doors.

> "Exceed your customer's expectations
> if you do, they'll come back over and over.
> Give them what they want - and a little more."
> - Sam Walton

The business people I talk to tell me that they are trying to provide better convenience and ease of access to their product and services. They agree that customer relationships, outside of pricing alone, will be the key to long-term survival. I find no reason to disagree.

Management

According to Levine (2017), both senior managers and stakeholders face a glut of information every business day. So how do leaders effectively corral efforts to improve their companies or organizations? Setting up internal processes, to segregate incoming information may be necessary. An example might be: As communication information officers (CIO)s and their staff grapple with the information glut, much of what they must do is decipher the myriad of data and channel the information to the divisions most impacted by said knowledge. By doing so, you save executives time and effort so they focus only on parsed and disseminated information that pertain primarily to them.

Systematic parsing of information was not ignored by AdviceNow (2019), who believed one of the key management practices used so that management doesn't spend too much time deciphering information, is proper dissemination. By focusing on what information effects current employees, and directing that information to provide solutions for senior leaders, becomes critical in today's informational environment. As an example, senior corporate strategists might require the following HR information: According to Toossi (2016), the labor participation rates are changing and they will for your company too. Teenagers and young adults, those 16-19 years old and 20-24 years old respectively, have been declining for quite a few decades and that trend is likely to continue through 2060. The primary labor force, those adults who are 25-54 years old, will continue to decline slightly as they have since the 1990s. The labor force participation rates for current employees 55+ had been on the increase since 1996, but since then it has been on the decline since 2012, and projections are that trend will continue. However, the 55+ age group as a whole (current 55+ and future 55+) will grow in numbers until the majority retire and depart from the labor force. [See Chap 2]. However, that information means little, at least initially, to the transportation manager. Human resources may evaluate that information and compare it to their company workforce, and the local demographics first, to anticipate hiring and training needs. That information is not likely to impact the transportation manager until the transportation manager requires an employee fill and then requires the assistance of the HR section to provide for the vacancy.

In that sense, the information manager acts as the communication clearing house for your organization. As the CIO directly reports to the senior manager, the information can be checked against the strategic intent of the organization. The C suite, (C staff), then organizes a cohesive plan to achieve better operational successes. Once the C staff sees how the senior operates along the lines of information sharing, they too matriculate their information to the middle-managers. At this point, positive movement on the profitability scale depends on how employees see the middle-management reaction, to the senior's information. The middle-management team should provide the same direction, and entice workers to see how they fit into the bigger picture and why they and their grouped individuals, are important to the communicative process.

In the above case, the CIO, or his/her counterpart, acts to direct information coming into the company and leads from the front. Additionally, he or she adds to support the process steps that lead to the aligned HR procedures of the employees. Once the employees understand that linkage, it helps them to see their own potential while adding to the company or organizational profits.

Understanding how the employee satiates the linkage between process and their job procedures, often requires explanation and practice. Managing several groups or activities within companies is not a simple task. Individual groups have their own way of adapting to the environment that affects them directly, within their respective environments. Each part of your company could represent a silo typically resulting from the practice, development, and adoption of procedures that work for them. However, as a senior leader or stakeholder, your attempts to problem solve and then leading from a silo, is seldom productive.

Also, what once worked well yesterday, may not work today, nor may it support future growth. Some will, but also accept that some will not. Further, change is most often successful when middle-managers engender their senior leader's and stakeholder's beliefs, and when silos soften and begin working in a collaborative manner, and learn from one another. When senior management, stakeholders, and middle-management lead a company or organization to practice systems organization and management, it is also a time to think larger and allow yourself and the middle-managers subordinate to your positions, to realize their own potentials and grow too.

So, what does this mean to the world of business management? What can it mean to the business economy, nationally? As posited by Toossi (2016), the overall long-labor force participation projections (by age, gender, race, and ethnicity) will decline through 2024, but it will also remain level afterwards through 2060. [See Chap 2]. However, according to Statista (2020), the U.S. gross domestic product (GDP) will increase from over 21.22 trillion from 2019 to nearly 32 trillion dollars by 2030. Given these statistics it seems likely that as the labor participations decrease and the GDP increase that more emphasis will be put into technologies that exact more profits. [See Chap 3].

These statistics seem as if they should be in the HR's primary lane right? Yes, and no. How do these figures affect company or organizational policy, sales and manufacturing operations, social and political environments, and competitive environments? According to Kaplan and Norton (2006), the bottom line is building the organization's human capital is everyone's responsibility, but only 19% of management integrate their human capital with their strategic ends. Without the lens that everyone is involved, the effort fails. Associatively, how do those figures and business outlooks effect marketing efforts, intra-inter communications, the readiness for your organization to adjust, equipment and technology, and your overall processes (both administrative and operational)? Companies should review where they are currently, in order to know the better paths toward their futures.

Leadership

Senior managers understand that only through shaping the spirit, ideological direction, and culture of an organization can they and their middle-managers provide a baseline so that the company can be understood by employees and customers. As a team, they can effectively manage an organization through the delegation of their duties to middle-managers through policy, processes, and procedures alignment. However, to sustain those alignments they must be practiced daily and companywide.

While this managerial oversight can be achieved using a 10k-30k foot lens, senior leaders, with a pragmatic mind set, realize that lens can be fogged by time, and require a periodic review. Also, indirect management can be lessened, if all middle-managers and employees take pride and ownership of their jobs, so that oversight becomes personal to them. That is one of the reasons the CCIM Three-Leg Stool was developed.

Also, most managers and leaders share common tenets – but they are not exactly alike. The timing for each is a learned trait, and not all master it. Without senior leadership involvement and management support, the chances for company or organizational continuous improvement are unlikely. According to Span (2019), the lack of trust is the largest challenge in today's companies, as it complicates and exacerbates divisional interaction for both senior and subordinate leaders. It is important that senior managers understand the significance of proposed changes from the lenses of the middle-management and lead divisions, within their organizations. Proposed changes should permeate the entire company to include gauging the understanding and subsequent actions of each middle-manager. Once accomplished, change and continuous improvement communications must also allow feedback, from the entire middle-manager groups.

Therefore, to engender trust, the goal of every senior manager should be to involve all middle-managers in the organization. This is true, if at all possible, no matter how much the middle-manager is involved in day-to-day decisions of managing the company, or not. Faulty or incomplete communication, does not engender trust. Examples of these types of failures were demonstrated within United States Joint Forces Command (USJFCOM). There were far too many siloes developed through discombobulated loyalties, which lead to diverse and ineffective reporting processes and procedures. Additionally, feedback for proposed changes was inadequate due to processes that allowed gatekeeping which disallowed adequate oversight. Attempts to re-organize failed. Further, while restoring trust was later attempted, too much dis-trust had already occurred.

> "When the trust account is high, communication is easy, instant, and effective."
> - Steven Covey

From the leadership perspective, it is essential that every middle-manager, who has a senior manager to report to and also subordinate employees, understand their responsibilities and their part in any change and continuous improvement process. This understanding is complete when those middle-managers know why it is important to them personally, why it is important to their team, and why it is important to the long-term survival of the company. Commonly, and when professionally led, I see this developed understanding most often in the order described, but not always.

Also, when discussing change management [See Chap 10] with some senior leaders and board members, I sometimes hear that they do not like confrontation with their subordinate managers or employees. Who does? However, as posited by Senge (2006), while some senior leaders may not relish some conflict, it is better to communicate openly so that seedlings of trust can be sown and resolutions to challenges might be found, early.

Further, when communicating early and openly, management can protect those who may be vulnerable, because fears can sometimes overshadow judgement. I have seen this happen, and leaders are usually some of the last ones to become aware of it, until after the damage has occurred. This deflection or diversion might come from someone who might wish to side-step a responsible solution through dis-unifying change and improvement, and by resorting to one-ups-man-ship, or promoting gossip, or even diverting from the truth, due to their own fears.

Sometimes it is not easy to overcome fear, or be comfortable. [See Chap 10]. If your goal is to re-establish trust and efficiencies in companies or organizations, management must first accept the reality to adopt a self-less attitude. To accomplish trust, it must be demonstrated by the senior leader first, so that subordinate leaders and managers can emulate it. As depicted by Harter (2019), how the middle-manager's experience the senior leader's resolve when branding that managerial concept is important, so that they can provide ongoing communications that promote and hold employees accountable with purpose. Also, the middle-manager's experience must be analogous to the employee's experience, so that the development of people and the survival of the company or organization becomes more important to both of them. It is when subordinate management sees that changes are important to the senior leader, that they begin to see their part in that orchestrated alignment, and move in the right direction toward effective change and continuous improvement management.

Associatively, it is important to accept that any change in your organization has the potential to affect other areas of your company. Those adjustments may have been unintended to improve one distinct area of the organization, and instead make it harder for others in the not-to-distant long-run. It is important to reiterate that systems management is not a snapshot of individual silos within companies, nor is it a snapshot of individuals running them, or the employees within them. Instead, systems management represents the combination and co-dependency of all of them.

Systems management focuses on the strategic operations, and the resulting increased profits associated with those combinations. Subsequently, senior leaders should periodically review all areas of the company or organization, and should guide and support the efforts of the corporate whole, in order for the management of systems to be sustainable. Further, those supported efforts must deny your competition's efforts to take over your market segment, and make sense to your customers or clients and supported by senior and middle-managers actions to support them.

As an example, I was personally blessed early on in my retail career to be present when the most senior leader in my organization, Mr. Sam Walton, and a middle-manager, store manager, had a conversation about leadership. Mr. Sam went to an area of the store with myself and the store manager trailing him, and opened the conversation by addressing the department manager. Hello, Ruth how are you doing? Fine, Mr. Sam came the reply. Ruth, how long have you been with Wal-Mart? Well, I think it was the Spring of 1965. Mr. Sam replied, "Well, you were one of our very first employees, I believe it might have been the Fall of 1964." "I believe your right, it was the Fall of '64", came the reply. "Well, Ruth the SKUs are all pulled forward, signs are up, its orderly, clean, and merchandized right." Then his tone softened even more…and he said, "Ruth, I am sure glad you are still with us here at Wal-Mart"! At this point, if Ruth could have glowed, she would have! "Take good care, Ruth", stated Mr. Sam as he walked away.

However, the lesson wasn't over. Mr. Sam, the middle-manager, and I walked around the counter and Mr. Sam looked directly into that middle-manager's eyes and asked, "What just happened? What did it cost us? And what did we gain?" The middle-manager was not a people person, I knew it, and Mr. Sam knew it, and he was trying to mentor him through an example. Many people skills were exemplified that day. Among those were personalization, earned affirmation, ownership, and management responsiveness.

Pragmatic senior leaders know that leading an organization, is not simply managing it. Senior managers must inculcate the company vision into each of your stakeholders and managers. [See Chap 4]. Leaders should constantly ask themselves, if their policies and benefits associated with those policies are experienced by everyone in the company Gandhi (2018). Once managers accept their leadership roles, that doesn't mean they will know how to do it. Sometimes senior managers must show and lead them. Senior leader oversight can produce a systemic and sustainable organizational vision providing employees with loyalty towards their organization, so they might be happier and stay longer. Retention and the loss of resources surrounding it, is a major issue in today's companies. [See Forward].

As posited by Patrick and Sundaram (2018), turnover, if policies and procedures are not systematically reviewed and comprehended, can hinder accomplishment of organizational results. Typically, those day-to-day and week-by-week resource losses can amount to more than many in organizations think about. However, it has been our experience those challenges often remain hidden, but they can also be high.

Contingency Planning

Every manager should also provide a baseline of defense for the possibility of contingent environments, which can affect every facet of business whether local or international and are frankly out of their control. The *what if* form of contingency planning might sound a bit far-fetched for some, but not for many - especially now. Catastrophic economic environment planning should represent a chapter in the company's playbook. Just as the business workplace struggles with the environments previously listed, each with their own business impact, there is another – but it is also thankfully rare.

As I reduce thought to digitizing this manuscript, the entire globe is reeling from the COVID-19 pandemic. The Covid-19 infection rates and the deaths associated with it are climbing daily. Even those not infected are certainly impacted by the current pandemic. Companies everywhere are struggling to stay afloat. Many are looking to find new ways to attract, retain, and provide their customers with products and services on-line because they cannot open their physical doors.

Employee health issues and economic stresses for businesses is at the forefront of almost every business conversation. Bringing people back to work safely and providing the transportation, raw materials, and so on play into every decision to produce both goods and services. Keeping employees safe relieves stress and helps them remain focused and engaged. [See Chap 2/Engaged vs. Disengaged]. As posited by Singh (2020), providing information in the workplace that emphasizes the health and safety measures enacted should be shared so that employees feel important to the company is an imperative during such health crises.

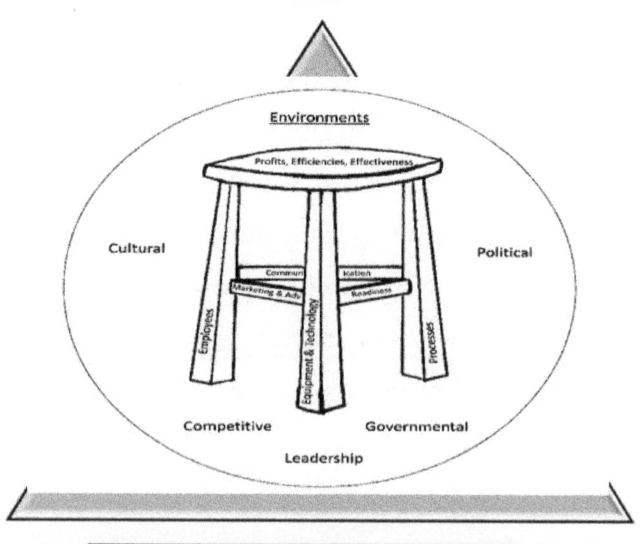

Chapter 10 – Change and Continuous Improvement Management

What is change and continuous improvement management (CCIM)? What is the difference between change management and CCIM? When should CCIM be used? How do companies or organizations develop supporters for CCIM? When shouldn't CCIM be used? All good questions, and all deserve good answers. So, let us take a pragmatic stab at explaining these in this section.

According to Ratenjee (2018), leaders expend enormous resources to influence changing their organizations. However, statistics represented by Ewenstein (2015), suggested that even when management is invested in change, that fewer than 30% of those efforts are sustained. Change management represents only the middle ground, if sustainment and continuous improvement is the goal. Change management acts as the conduit for updating performance and making it part of the culture, represented by continuous improvement. Challenges are many and change and continuous improvement management is hard, so why do we do it? Because the outcomes are worth it! It is often the efforts enacted through CCIM that reveal where the organization is failing. Also, it is quite often not comprehended by the stakeholders of the company until too late, otherwise.

Simple change management efforts, in the context to make changes in one area to make it better, is just that. The focus is usually to improve one or two areas within the company or organization. However, change and continuous improvement management goes further. The primary goal for the CCIM is to change the company or organization in a pragmatic way that allows management to look across organizational policy, processes, and procedures with a systematic focus to support long-term and sustainable futures through continuous improvements. Change management, not CCIM, will provide transverse input's to parts of the company. Change and continuous improvement management takes change management and introduces ways to infuse continuous improvement by weaving thought processes throughout management's decision processes, thereafter.

Visionary CCIM leadership should emulate the creation of new or different organizational goals, not merely solve problems. Professionally administered CCIM allows the preferred outcomes to adhere to companies and organizations with resilient, adoptive, and genuine transformation. According to Gravells (2006), both short and long-term strategies must meld, to make actionable change occur. Also, transforming naysayers into supporters, while learning why they originally disliked the change, is both strategic and positive for the organization. Some of those stresses are growing pains and should be rationalized as growth. Management should not allow themselves to be swayed by appeasing what does not fit the overall organizational goals. The goal for CCIM should be to enhance and sustain them.

Change and continuous improvement management represents both training tools and sustainment processes. Training tools should then act as a gateway to the development and guidance for management to make decisions that change, improve, and then sustain a company's or organization's current and future standing. That strategy may be to improve internal or external operations, and or profits. Change management can utilize many operational vehicles to bring it to fruition, including: Policy and procedure alignments across the business enterprise, process or re-process engineering, internal training systems, management meetings, company survey information, professional consultants, company newsletters, or combinations of these to achieve success.

> "If you want truly to understand something, try to change it."
> - Kurt Lewin

Most managers know that the old top-down methods of change management no longer work. They are right. They don't. Why don't we take a different attitude? Almost all sustainable change takes place where management and workers understand their efforts toward change. Change managers should work directly with the most senior manager, so that pushback from those who challenge change can be managed responsibly and pragmatically. Tams (2018), and Kotte (1996), indicated that organizational change is orchestrated best from the necessary direction of the CEO, and the matriculation and buy-in of middle-managers and employees. Providing a clear end-state, and listening as organizational change takes place, is paramount to actionable change results. From a management perspective, dialogue, meaning the suspension of judgement and the lessening of emotional judgement, should take the place of *must win* attitudes. When dialogue displaces discussion, and black and white understandings become a richer shade of gray, it works much better. Done properly *must wins* can turn into *win wins*. [See Chap 7].

When company stakeholders realize they need to make changes to stay competitive, senior management should identify what and where those changes are required, and by when they need to occur. Some of those changes may be internal business or operational policy adjustments and may include change in job descriptions, a change in technologies, process and procedure alignments, communication shortfalls, employee diversification, change in supplier, a change in distribution of goods or services, a change to support a different customer, or a change in management within different divisions of the company. [See Chap 7]. Disruptions, in any of these, can affect the business or operational integrity of a company.

Senior management and stakeholders have the responsibility to identify what steps may be necessary to actualize provisions for safeguards, against those changes. Also, senior managers must decide, if the division or organization is prepared for change. Some will be more malleable to change than others. The change and continuous improvement process will have varying degrees of both abstract and concrete perceptions between divisions or the middle-managers, who also lead employees. As discussed by Santos and Garcia (2006), the mental models of group leaders need to align with the change and improvement management processes. They should see how the change process will benefit themselves, their individual group, and the company so that they see and understand that the effort will not be wasted. Therefore, the CCIM objectives are affected by the behaviors of others. When understanding displaces fear, changes can occur. Fear makes fixed goals difficult.

This concept is further explained by Todnem By, et al. (2018), with their Organizational Team-Individual-Change (OTIC) concept. Their concept involves the team in the change and continuous improvement process. Each team has their own individual cultures and concepts of how change will affect their unit or division. Involving each group in the change and continuous improvement process, helps change gain a foothold toward sustainability.

For senior managers, knowing the priority of which area of the business or organization requires change to support the entire company, is important. Further, it is critical to know who is more malleable, or least likely to be able, to provide leadership to help make those changes. That deductive assessment provides information, which may allow seniors to appraise which division leaders are more adaptable to change, and may prime the field for positive change sooner. Not underestimating this assessment is essential, because priming the field for change can lead directly to the successful implementation of the change and continuous improvement management process.

Most CCIM efforts, enacted by senior and middle-managers, are iterative in nature. That is, they study where their organizations are failing and attempt to change only a smaller part of the organization while minimizing the second and third order affects that might change with those iterative options. Done this way, CCIM efforts can decrease disruptions and enhances the chance for successes, not only in the management effort, but also in the buy-in from employees. Adopting a pragmatic iterative CCIM effort within the organization, enhances future and further changes successes and the sustainment habits that are the ultimate goals for the long-term.

Learning to adjust to a newer way of doing things, will always involve risk. As described by Kotter (1996), companies can decrease risk at an exponential rate when the most senior management and direct supporters understand, and are supportive of the changes necessary. Because some mid-level managers, and some employees, where promoted by emulating their predecessor's steps, they view their continued successes depend on the duplication of their predecessor's beliefs and actions, in order to move upward. Some of those duplicated actions and beliefs have now become comfortable for them. There exists more risk in comfort, if that comfort results in complacency.

According to Kaplan and Norton (2006), change is perpetual, and the organization which was aligned once will be mis-aligned later. It is a normal occurrence. This is not to suggest all things will need to change, some will not, and others may need to remain static while other iterative changes take place. However, subversion of the CCIM focus occurs when senior management allows stalwarts to sway thinking, that is meant to manipulate and cement more comfortable stalwart positions. In short, complacencies result in not moving. Not moving means your competition may soon outpace your company. Change and continuous improvement management sets the tone and direction for companies and organizations to remain competitive.

For this reason, CCIM consultants are far more successful when they work directly with the CEO and senior management staff.

Middle-managers must see senior management's efforts to change. Many employees will follow the middle-management's guidance, but they can also become confused if the guidance from the senior and middle-manager varies too much. The directions from too many leaders, especially when they don't agree, exacerbates the change efforts. Matrix directions and the change management process focused toward continuous improvement are not friends, when this occurs.

There may be a few employees who may not accept change, and will hinder benchmark change and continuous improvement efforts. When push-back occurs, senior management should realize it is a natural occurrence. However, enough push-back can thwart efforts and derail forward movement, so that change efforts might not have opportunities to reset a more proactive workforce. Sidebar conversations, which might become emotional, should not interfere with the focus towards continuous improvement. The fewer outside distractions, the better. [See Chap 7]. That is one reason why streamlining communication between the senior management and change agents is crucial. Seeing the relationship between the change agent and senior management helps maintain the importance of the change and continuous improvement process, because if it is important to the boss - it is important to the middle-managers and to the company.

An example might help. Mike Roberts was an experienced change agent and was hired by a company that had just experienced some dismantling of their supervisory structure. From the staff's perspective, there was little explanation for the change that was abruptly enacted by senior management. One level of management had been divided into two, and animosities grew between the two once-peer groups, as one part of the group now answered to another. To make matters worse, both groups were heavily engaged in daily operations which demanded much of their time. The lead supervisor was far too busy to oversee the change process and focused on his operational reports directly to the CEO of the company.

The CEO completely relied on the staff to investigate the need for new improvement efforts. Also, the CEO focused on battling his nearby competitor, so he was not focused on improving staff interactions. Yet, both he and his management leads knew something had to be done, because communications and some operational aspects of the company were broken and inefficient. He was simply unaware of the turmoil within his own company.

Mike Roberts asked the lead supervisor what he wanted to accomplish. The lead manager for the CCIM knew he should be involved, but he was also not sure how much he wanted to be since it didn't seem to be a priority with the CEO. So, he told Roberts that he should go to find out what changes may be needed, if they were needed, and let him know. Roberts talked to key lead segments of the company and after nearly four months he had identified six key primary nodes of change that were needed to obtain and improve cohesive efficiencies and communicative systems within the organization.

Iterative reports were sent to the lead manager every week explaining who, what, when, where, why, and how communication and operational disconnects were observed. While Roberts had been sending regular reports to the lead, the lead had allowed many of those who would have to reconstruct their efforts to improve operations, to intercept those reports and then pass the reports to him.

Therefore, a primary flaw existed as the lead middle-manager had allowed those who would have to change individual operations, to also be the gatekeepers of reports and information passed on to him. Hence, Roberts had no idea if some, or none, of those reports were received by the lead manager. Exacerbating the situation further, the lead middle-manager was not involved, and his staff noted his reluctance to become involved, the communications were dissected by an unhappy and complacent staff, and the feedback mechanisms were close to non-existent. So, both the purpose and scope of the CCIM were poorly supported and therefore misunderstood. Consequently, the CCIM effort failed.

While it is of the utmost importance that the CCIM agent directly works with the most senior manager during the CCIM effort, it is also important to allow the change agent to interface directly with the middle-managers and employees. The CCIM agent's relationship with those who actually perform the tasks of work, is also important. If the middle-managers and employees know they can discuss any topic in confidence – unless the communication reveals illegal or threatening intent for another worker – without those comments being revealed, they can and usually will provide important information. [See quantitative and qualitative in this Chap, below].

Focusing on small change improvement wins, and celebrating them helps incremental change and adaptation towards the change in the company culture. [See Chap 9-Management and Employee Relationships]. It is important to remember that each incremental change may affect other parts of CCIM system. So, before changing something analyze how that change could affect other areas in your organization. To mitigate risks, senior management and stakeholders should review what second and third level affects those changes may inject into the company or organization elsewhere. What changes are laudable? Which will better the chance for a positive return on investment (ROI), and what changes might bring the most risk to the company?

Also, Kotter (1996) posited that paring down to the essentials of business successes, can take time and effort. Once change occurs, it will require constant reminders through management, until the culture changes so that regression does not occur. Management's support of the CCIM efforts, can allow the changes to cement in place. Further, if the data gathered to provide guidance for the CCIM efforts are organized and meaningful, the grounded and focused results are worth it. When orchestrated pragmatically, the change can provide longevity for the company or organization.

As stated earlier, there will be challenges to change. Internal impingements to CCIM include: solutions that are not originating from inside the business, fear, and distrust. Each are closely associated with one another, but are also definitive in nature for members of your staff or employees. Ideas for continuous improvement, when the ideas do not originate from within the organization, can sometimes stem from feelings of not being creative enough to show the boss he or she could have been more forward thinking – but wasn't. General fear from employees may be portrayed through anxiety of how the boss will react to such revelations, and what the boss's reaction to those revelations may mean. [See Chap 7]. Will the boss think less of me, my team, or both? Also, distrust can occur when the creator of the improvement might seem to upstage the current manager or staff, whether real or imagined.

Using a mixed-methods, quantitative and qualitative approach to survey analysis, many of the pitfalls to the CCIM efforts are revealed. [See quantitative and qualitative in this Chap, below]. Pitfalls may occur when the managers adopt changes that include adding processes and procedures to the business that doesn't fit the corporate policy itself. According to Bray (2017), those ill-adopted attempts might include adding an inexperienced transitional CCIM lead and not integrating the changes management wishes to develop into something the business can support, or adopting initial technologies that lead nowhere after the first blush of trials just because it seems expedient.

> "The combination of qualitative and quantitative approaches provide a more complete understanding of a research problem than either approach alone."
> - John Creswell

Also, it is important to review the progress of change implementation as they occur, across the organization. According to Kotter (1996), there are eight typical mistakes change initiators make when trying to change companies or organizations. They are: (1) Allow too much complacency. Tomorrow, or because it is initially harder, is not be used as an excuse, (2) deficiency when creating an adequately dominant managing coalition, (3) undervaluing the strength of vision, (4) vastly under-communicating that vision, (5) allowing blockages to support the updated or improved vision, (6) failing to establish short-term triumphs, (7) announcing success too quickly, and (8) forgetting to secure changes steadfastly into the company, or organizational culture. Understanding the challenges before senior and middle-management starts the CCIM efforts, allow better orchestration and can off-set fears before they manifest.

These challenges and their associated emotions are further supported by Kotter (1996), who believed blocking change and improvement efforts are typically demonstrated through characteristics of employee obstinance or fear of the change. He posited that there are three internal company and organizational characteristic types that suspend or deny improvement. These were egoistic managers who may over-estimate their present accomplishments and competitive stance, listen inadequately, and understand with a laissez-faire attitude.

Also, internally fixated employees may have challenges comprehending the forces that exist, therefore they overlook menaces and are not open to prospects for improvement. Further, administrative cultures can stifle individuals who desire to react to fluctuating business or economic opportunities, and may thwart management efforts. Knowing where and when these internal challenges exist, can greatly increase success rates for change and continuous improvement efforts. [See Chap 2, Chap 3 & Chap 7].

Also, it is important for senior managers to explain to middle-managers that the CCIM process will result in some mistakes. Those mistakes should be forgivable, but also those mistakes should be focused toward learning new ways to be competitive. This belief is supported by WD-40's President/CEO Garry Ridge (2018), who posited that learning is about distinguishing between an affirmation, or undesirable consequence, of an act. Ridge did not focus on punishment. His efforts to change his organization, were to encourage organizational wide offerings and involve his employees to do it. He believed in including the employee's ideas and creative abilities while improving current products and services. Further, Ridge believed by removing challenges for them it would help support WD-40's strategic focus. This is yet another reason to support a divisional review of policies, processes, and procedures to promote the overall vision and current policies to align with the parent organization.

Also, when the CCIM process is communicated, with a focus utilizing dialogue and without the importance of affixing blame, as compared to only discussion and blame, the deficits can be learned from and can result in more positive outcomes. [See Chap 7]. Switching the focus from *who - to why and when – to how* can be associated with change successes and for the continuous improvement of the company, and can transform into action more readily. As posited by Ratanjee (2018), when senior and middle-managers help employees see a better future the employees begin to work with more energy, enthusiasm, optimism, and higher commitment. Employee standards can be expected and upheld, but also how those standards are adjudicated by management, has value.

Further, emphasis to support how CCIM implementations can work in companies and organizations are championed by TenSix (2017), and supported by Yemm (2007). Their shared emphasis advocated ideas that senior management, whom may believe they know what and how to support the delivery and the mission of CCIM itself, need to be improved. Once the analysis is completed, they are often surprised. Management usually discover that their efforts to explain the tangible benefits to teams, the funding aspects required, the buy-in to improve the lack of stakeholder involvement, the communication improvements needed to provide consistency, and the adaptability required are critical to sustaining continuous improvements have identifiable gaps. The discovery of those surprises, can deter future resource losses. Also, they may help steer improvements through involvement, communication, and buy-in by breaking down the barriers that management were not otherwise aware, existed.

Regardless of the challenges CCIM brings to the company, its benefits far outweigh the risks, because not keeping up with business environments and cultures result in companies being outpaced and can usually result in eventual business closures. According to Danziger (2019), more than 75,000 retail stores, both large and small, will close by 2026 and the trend is expected to continue. As big box stores continually feel pressures to close, and more of their products are offered via the internet, the processes to bring the product to the electronic stores will be the next challenge for management.

As senior business stakeholders and professional change agents grapple with these disastrous numbers, what can be done to off-set their business risks? The future belongs to the businesses sectors that can over-ride competitor's technological solutions. Otherwise, customers who enjoy the benefits technology brings will link themselves to products and services those technologies provide access to. A way to compete when not completely up to date with technology is people skills. As championed by Madsen (2019), the soft skills will become more important.

Further, companies will want to retain the best employees to produce, retain one-stop quality, and to transport those goods directly to the consumer. Regardless of the artificial intelligence, or machined solutions, the technologies alone will not provide the human element which includes person-to-person communication, acute thinking solutions, inventive strategies, and innovative concepts required of many future purchasers of goods and services. In short, if goods are purchased more often via the internet, overcoming the inability for shoppers to experience touch prior to purchase, competing companies will need to provide greater personal guarantees and follow-up for their offerings.

This book helps management evaluate those risks, and promotes the provision of pragmatic solutions to move closer towards managing change and profitable adjustments. Also, it provides management with concepts which might increase worker loyalty and longevity and prevent a competitor to utilize their advantages to steal your company's or organization's market. An instantaneous mandate and action for all businesses and organizations, is to adopt a broader lens that heightens the focus on the changing customer's desires.

As supported by Hamel and Prahalad (1996), who surmised that during the CCIM process, it is important to include all the players in an orchestrated way so that alignment of effort solidifies. Here, the focus should be to obtain cohesion between both the divisional managers and employees, so both feel involved and valued. Acceptable risks occur, when those positive outcomes outweigh the effort and costs of the change and continuous improvement management expansions.

Both micro and macro (tactical and strategic) changes should be considered. According to Farnam Street (2018), micro changes toward a future macro end state, is always the best option. The operational, tactical, and the stakeholder strategic change efforts may conflict. Both might be impacted by the environment in different ways. Subsequently, it is important that senior management discover which managers and employees are the more flexible to achieve both tactical and strategic goals. [See Chap 2]. Gauging how managers and employees adjust can be accomplished through periodic dialogue. [See Chap 7].

Also, Brest (2010), discussed that not all parts of an organization will need to be tactical or strategic, at any one time. Change and improvement processes aimed at strategic end results can operate independently, and at different times, to meet business or organizational cycles. Therefore, the senior management should help the organizational leaders understand what their goals, both tactical and strategic, are so they might more easily see how they fit into the process affecting the final outcome. Further, the change and continuous improvement agent must help leaders and stakeholders evaluate how different parts of the organization currently fit into the tactical or strategic goals of the organization. Planning and execution must be flexible, because different divisions of the organization may be focused on the tactical or the strategic, or both.

A practical and professional progressive plan by the senior leadership begins with what they are wanting to change. Second, leadership should review how the cross-pollination of the return on investment matriculates throughout the organization. The evaluation of the tactical and strategic change efforts correlate, (or do not) correlate, with one another to meet the environmental and cash flow requirements of the organization. These orchestrated changes will usually fall within phases and timelines.

A positive affirmation of the organization, and a clearly announced vision by the senior leader is important, so that both managers and employees understand why the vision is essential in order to reach milestones. According to Ratanjee (2018), the CEO of any organization, regardless if the organization's environment, or whether it seems stable or is poised for change, should continue to communicate a positive vision. According to Fleming and Witters (2012), communication efforts typically fail when employees reveal that a high of 73% - and all the way down to a low of 9% of them (depending on the industry) do not strongly agree that they understand what their organization stands for, and what makes them different from competitors. Why? Disjointed change management attempts which decry managerial and operational improvements are wrapped around old change and organizational models that do not work in today's business environments. Ratanjee goes on to posit that the basic reason for *communications failure* is [See Chap 8] the use of mechanical models of CCIM that stress the embodiment of centralization, predictable behaviors, and easy to discern outcomes. However, as environments constantly change, the organizations that need to change with them are not flexible enough to keep up with those types of models.

Employees are invaluable assets to the CCIM inputs. Therefore, it is important to inculcate the human elements in progressive change. These elements should include how families and communities will gain from the organization's business goals, whether those changes are divisional or company-wide. Subsequently, more collaboration and involvement with workforce groups is imperative for sustainable future businesses. As posited by Ratanjee (2018), mandated and top down and mandated traditional change iterations will fail at progressively faster rates. Also, working backwards from an ending desired state decreases anxiety. Pulling all middle-managers together so that aggregate strengths, challenges, and weaknesses of overall processes and procedures, punctuate much more resilient results. As resiliency becomes a purposeful and normal goal, continuous improvement becomes part of the culture.

Professional change and continuous improvement managers know that not everything new is good and not everything old is bad, and vice-versa. What matters are the environments faced by the companies and organizations that they attempt to improve. Associatively, finding purpose might be supported by opening dialogue, while focusing on what has worked in the past and see if it is worth revisiting. Then taking that information and moving it into action statements that are current and the strategic goals accompanying them make long-term sense.

Also, these action statements should not be a rose-colored approach, instead a way of achieving dialogue over discussion and vision over planning, first. Taking a problem focused approach usually only exacerbates the problem. As supported by Ratanjee (2018), using an approach that focuses on positive purpose statements, will do more than support problem solving. If senior managers and change agents focus on the promotion of new ideas, dreams, and a vision for the future, it often allows for creative solutions to stagnant challenges and helps positive change occur. Guide groups into advocacy by allowing co-dependent vision, missions, and values to be aired through dialogue and create ownership of those supporting goals towards your strategic vision. When subordinate managers and employees experience and feel personal ownership of their responsibilities, it creates work environments that require less oversight of employee actions and result in better efficiencies.

Re-Organize or Not?

In the attempt to readjust a company to meet challenges associated with (government, competitive, political, and so on) environments, some organizations or companies attempt to re-organize most, if not their entire, structures. Re-organizations are not always bad, and are not always good. According to Blakely-Gray (2019), some of the advantages to reorganizations can be increased profits, efficiency improvements, business or organizational longevity, recovered or enhanced strategies, and financial reclamations. Some of the disadvantages include: failure, reduction of morale, perplexed customer or clients, substantial loss of time, and losses in revenue.

These opportunities and risks can be mitigated, through the pragmatic analysis of the company or organization. Here are some of mitigation opportunities we have discovered. First, senior leaders must accept that changing organizations and the culture within them takes time. According to Freeland (2018), staged tactical change aimed toward realistic strategies work best, and are implemented from the top down with a few orchestrators responsible for the pace and operational tie-ins. While there may be necessity to change quickly for some areas, it is not always wise to push change to the degree that it is unsustainable across the organization.

Second, keeping up with constant change can be unmanageable if attempts at re-organization happen too often. According to the University of East Anglia (2016), if workers experience re-organizations too often, they lose faith in their ability to grow within that same organization. Additionally, as depicted by Heidari-Robinson and Heywood (2016), communication is a key factor in reorganizing any business, whether to or from a geographical, customer, or mixed segmented basis. [See Chap 7]. Some of the primary reasons for failed re-organizations are challenges associated with employee changes, insufficient and poorly allocated resources, prolonged distraction and loss of productivity, the supervisors who challenge change, and what the organization chart depicts is not what people do. [See Chap 2]. Also, some failures are associated with frustrated workers who leave due to the re-organization, or the attempts of re-organization, and the unforeseen changes that disrupt operations. [See Chap 9].

Phased re-organizations help to correct many of these challenges, but also the communications must be clear to each part of the company. [See Chap 7]. Senior managers and stakeholders should realize that re-organizations are organizational transformations and are resultant of changes which must be communicated from multiple viewpoints, as those communications must be understood, composed, and enacted by many internal managers and operator employees.

According to Gravells (2006), employees who resist change commonly come with their own fears, emotions, and irrationalities they believe to be true. They have their own established 'mental models' and seek to comprehend what has happened before. Even the establishment of trust takes time. The more fears, emotions, and irrationalities exist, the longer it will take. Therefore, the ability to assuage middle-managers and employees should be at the top of soft skill attributes portrayed by senior managers.

Third, change efforts are hard for senior managers, but are also much harder for middle-managers. It is most often the middle-manager who will bear the brunt of the change within his or her division. He or she must readjust the culture, which has been built over time, in order to enact change more directly with those who actually complete the work. The subordinate manager should focus on explaining why the change is beneficial, to the whole of his or her group or unit.

After the frustration of attempting change to meet the expectations of the senior manager happens often enough, the subordinate managers begin to take shortcuts as they realize the next senior manager will change their operational functions anyway. This is one of the many reasons for USJFCOM's failure. [See Chap 1 & Chap 9]. This is truly a trickle-down effect from the most senior leader throughout the organization's management chain, and if not administered and supported correctly, it can lead to mayhem. From the employee's viewpoint it may be more likely they will either not make the change or begin subtle change - to appease senior managers, than to put much effort in the actual change requested.

However, the challenge to re-organize is not insurmountable, but also the effort to acquire a successful re-organization requires a very pragmatic view of the company or organization prior to the attempt. Capitalizing on existing strengths and involving your management team is a good place to start. As changes unfold, it is not usually necessary to throw out what is working. Instead, see how much of what is working can be added to the changes that must be made. The re-organization should enhance what is working for the benefit of the whole organization, and shed what does not.

Solicited survey information, which do not reveal the name of the survey participant, can be used to aggregate important viewpoints can be helpful, and are usually a cheaper alternative than trying to ascertain information without them. That is one of the reasons managers often opt to use surveys. However, using only one type of survey, either quantitative or qualitative alone, can give organizations incomplete and misleading data. At this point, and according to Mckim (2017), the decisions should include the acceptance that the use of both quantitative and qualitative results can give the true picture of how those existing programs or processes might be added or deleted, so as to support and not to detract from the necessity of change.

Quantitative and Qualitative Methods

Simple organizational studies to ascertain how management and employees work to maintain operational efficiencies, often do not work. In fact, they can even be harmful. Typically, those studies only provide a snapshot of the current circumstances, but also do not reveal what could be. I believe a better alternative is the mixed methods survey approach. The reason that both quantitative and qualitative combination (mixed) studies can reveal more than quantitative or qualitative alone, is that the quantitative can tell management the strength of the *what* answers to questions asked of the organization and the qualitative reveals *why* those numbers have meaning and what they represent through the lens of their employees. Incorporating a mixed methods approach to surveys can give a far deeper understanding of the current organization and helps management focus on rational sustainable change. Attitudes, and sometimes challenges, can be revealed when mixed employee data and viewpoints are compared and contrasted. The right questions, when juxtaposed to one-another, provide revelations that can be compelling.

Cultural

Cultural adaptations, whether they include ethnic, race, gender, or age, are those adaptations that work for the group in question. These are natural occurrences, because cultures simply develop when something works well, i.e., a process, particular technology, training, etc., for a specific group over time. There is nothing wrong with that, unless that segregated work group detracts from the efficiencies or effectiveness of another sister group working in the same organization and results in siloed operations. Engle (2013) posited that some siloed cultures will have to change significantly to support the entire operational enterprise, so that efficiencies and resource protection can be realized. Many cultures will not need to change, and some may require significant re-organization.

Siloed operational cultures may not seem like a big problem, at first. Generally, they are obscured by just getting basic job requirements accomplished within the organization. However, as management dig into the output and the effects those siloes have on your operation, it becomes evident your company is slowly being robbed of resources. As Hopp (2016), surmised, both the managers and leaders must align their efforts to be effective. The real danger here is the hidden natural losses, which can occur through individual siloes, could set a precedence in policy or operational processes that cannot be supported by your organization in the long-term.

> "Silos may be part of the culture."
> - Paul Engle

As independent units congeal into processes that work for those individual units, they can be easily overlooked by both senior and middle-management. Without a pragmatic analysis of those independent processes and procedures, their adoptions and acceptances can be harmful. So, care should be exercised before supporting erratic processes and procedures, before they gain purchase and so setting precedence is not achieved. [See Forward, Chap 6, Chap 9/Competitive Environments].

For instance, management's acceptance of a nuance in one area may lead to expectations that the same type of nuance should also be accepted and supported in another. Once the acceptance of that nuance occurs, another group within the organization may feel unappreciated or even slighted, should they not get the same approval. This group may consider themselves as part of the out-group, and are therefore mis-aligned. Pacheco and Webber (2016), calculated that employees who felt they were aligned with their company received more help to complete their tasks and more decision-making authorization than those who did not feel part of the organizational system. Associatively and subsequently, the acceptance of seemingly benign nuances can lead to employee separations.

As postulated by Schein and Schein (2019), operational and functional groups that develop internal cultures, can also be affected by shifts in leadership. That can be especially true, if leadership changes often. If senior leaders change often, the culture or cultures they supervise must change to support the new vision of the senior leader. What is important here is the turmoil represented in those changes, [See Chap 9] and how those changes are enacted and administrated. Even the greatest of hurdlers cannot follow rules if he or she is told to change shoes at every other hurdle, while attempting to win the race. These challenges also affect the military.

Similarities and Dis-similarities between Civilian Organizations and Military Organizations

Civilian and military organizations both have challenges to keep pace with their environments. In the business sense, they are more similar than dissimilar. In the operational sense they are more dissimilar than similar. In business, customers and clients vote with their feet. In the military, the tax payer agrees or disagrees with budgeted cost outlays for operations through governmental, political, and legislative pressures. Considerations usually include the tightening of budgets, even if distasteful for some, it may be necessary to make adjustments associated with cost, efficiencies, and effective output.

Similarities between both the civilian and military challenges are not often discussed, but should be. As posited by Korman and Klapper (1978), the necessity to meld the military and scholarly study was not lost to General Dwight D. Eisenhower, in 1946 when he was the Chief of Staff, who wrote a memorandum to the General and Special Staff Divisions of the Army, in which he supported combining those efforts during war and peace. Game Theory advocates rejoice! Great changes have occurred in the technologies, economies, and geo-political atmosphere we experienced since World War II, but also the decisional processes associated with Game Theory have remained generally true. Decisions made without a thorough understanding of internal and external technologies, economies, and the geo-political atmospheres are inter-connected and therefore concerns neither all military nor all made by scholarly interpretations.

However, there are also dissimilarities. The dissimilarities can sometimes cause conflict. One of the most difficult challenges for some civilian senior managers, who support the military with their products or services, is how their offerings can become obsolete, so quickly. While some civilian managers understand the challenges with product or services obsolescence, they may not understand the why, and how the military must sometimes operate the way they do.

A delivery of a standard civilian product, to support a military contract, can mean adjustments to the contract, the product, or both depending on the product or service components end use. Adjustments like these must change to fit the precise application of upgraded technologies made to compete with an emerging adversary's weapons or delivery systems. Further, those changes may also be branch specific.

As the military needs change, the contracts have to engender frequent flexibilities including modified work orders (MWO). While analysts attempt to foresee and contain such challenges through the applications, and flexibilities provided in the scopes of work (SOW), the compartmentalization of shared emerging technologies with military suppliers, and so on - not everything can be caught in time. Enemies of the U.S. will not simply wait on our convenience. To those who may not have the need to know, and certainly to those who shouldn't know, the acceptance of these types of things is paramount and must sometimes occur.

Also, some senior military managers may not believe they have competitors. I have seen this happen. The truth is, they do. Organizational enemies do not exist on the battlefields, alone.

Some military organizations are closed organizations, similar to closed business organizations. They begin to believe in their abilities to outlast their competitors, without the need to change. Thus, they become stagnant within their own walls. Inflexibilities occur internally, and they become increasingly stagnant outside of them.

> "The most important six inches on the battlefield …is between your ears."
> - James Mattis

Eventually, they begin to react too late to competitors who are awaiting their chance to surpass them. Subsequently, those competitors gain in profits or prestige to perform certain tasks, that the stagnated organization once performed well. As the military budget continues to shrink, also similar to civilian sector segments, profits or outputs usually provided and accepted by customers or clients begin to diminish due to competitors out-pacing and out-performing them. The government will simply have little choice, but to also require the military organizations to improve their operations, communication skills, and ability to contract future technologies or services more efficiently. Failure to do so enacts oversight. Eventually, military improvements become the responsibility of the Department of Defense and the Office of Management and Budget (OMB) for the provisioning for the nation's security. Further, the American taxpayer will demand it.

When organizations are comprised of military, government civilians, contractors, and civilian trained employees these challenges are more diverse and widespread. Sometimes, it can be due to divergent loyalties within the organization. It is normal for middle managers to be loyal to the bosses they serve. If the military member is still in uniform, he or she might obfuscate information from civilian contractors so that the senior military leader does not hear problems that the contractors ferret out. Sometimes that obfuscation might be connected to the military budget. Military leaders are typically understaffed, and must hire civilian staff to solve augmented problems. Sometimes the problems, which can be surfaced through either the military members or civilian contractors, do not have immediate solutions.

The more senior military member you are, the more you might realize that bringing problems to the military leader without possible solutions to solve them, does not make their job easier, nor yours. Only a thorough understanding of the policies, processes, and procedures can support the prioritization to meet those liquid preparations for wartime requirements. Properly adjudicated, those combinations can allow a baseline from which to adjust. The government civilian program was designed to help perform duties to support those contingencies.

The government civilian program is a graded and graduated program, whose employees can support either a civilian or military boss. By nature, their jobs are those of longevity. If the civilian is hired as a consultant, garnered through a military support contract, he or she is typically more likely to be loyal to that contractor, even if it sometimes means not bringing up something that the military bosses need to know. Bypassing confrontation, even if it is clear improvements can be made, can lead to personal longevity in the workplace.

If the primary lead of the contracting agency has the ability to decipher and facilitate those differences, that is great. If not, siloed operations can spell a slow death to the provision and sustained operational effectiveness and the sustainment of efficiencies of procedural training adjustments needed to support military operations. Improvements can be lost due to the frustrations of inconsistencies between the contracting agencies and the military. If the civilian employees and the military do not have an open senior forum to discuss these differences and the best solutions to solve them, losses in the prestige, operational effectiveness, efficiencies and trust between these groups occur. Once less competitive environments between different contractor groups is lessened, the lead contractor, and his military counterparts, can obtain a modicum of dialogue with a peppering of respectful candor.

Organizations that train employees to share information and build trust, sometimes offer oversight groups to alleviate some of these inconsistencies. Doing so, is a good first step. However, the oversight group cannot be in name only, because the intricacies of gathering those critical pieces of information to increase effectiveness focused to build shared trust between segmented groups requires a degree of sophistication.

Also, like any other dialogue versus discussion group, those groups have to be administered and shared properly. Having group discussions, regardless of how the group shares its information with one another, is only as important as how it is shared and made actionable for the whole of the organization. If there is a gatekeeper involved with the discussion, or if the most senior leaders do not get to hear unbiased information from the oversight group, the effort is lost. Those meetings, or discussions, become a moot exercise. They become wastes of time, energy, the resources for the organization, and for all those who participate.

Due to the diversification of loyalties and protectionisms within organizations, which contain both civilian and military employees, gathering actionable information across both groups is challenging. However, even though these loyalties present those challenges, they are necessary to overcome, so that gaps are identified, to improve communication difficulties, and to build trust between each. For the civilian contracting companies, those gaps might be represented by the companies which must compete for contractual bids. For military lead organizations those gaps may be represented by differences in military and civilian loyalties associated with direct reports, relationships between contractor companies, and the feedback associated with senior forums - or the lack thereof.

Generally, when the CCIM efforts and challenges are compared across the senior lead civilian and military organizations, it is easier to see the similarities between those actions which are otherwise thought as dissimilar. Both must similarly consider the levels of management, employee diversity, feelings of superior/inferior treatment between segmented groups, and so on. However, in order to fully comprehend the challenges with differences in those dichotomies, we must discuss the differences associated with the military requirement to maintain the need for secrecy.

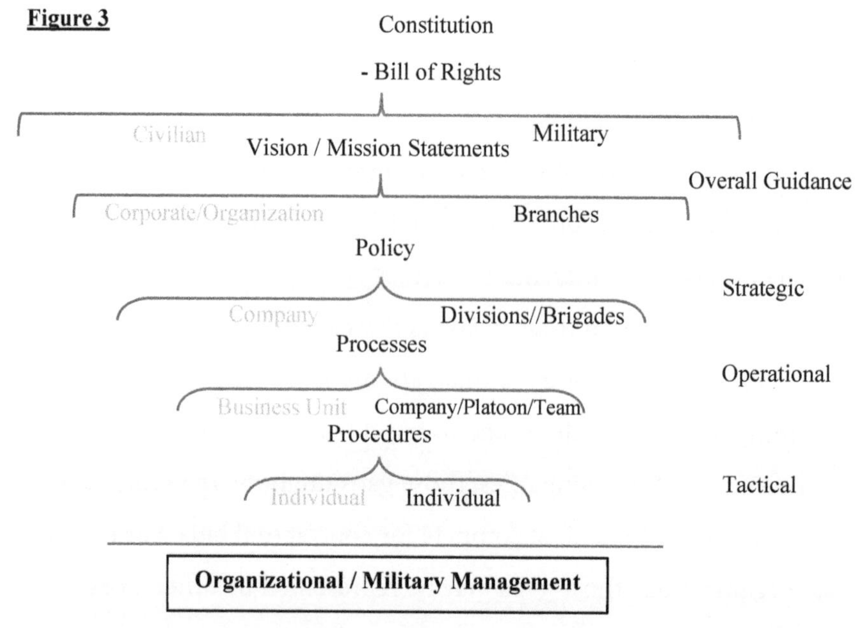

For those who have never been in the military, the closest civilian relative with the need for secrecy might be explained by the research and development (R&D) stages of products or services. In particular the military requirement for secrecy is similar with R&D skunkworks, which are planning operations usually located in remote locations where the most significant and secret developments or modifications to existing products, take place. The secrecy is meant to advance products or services, or to thwart competitor's advances. Although civilian organizations keep their R&D operations secret, similar to the military, the overall potential for life threatening secrets to emerge is typically, much less. Civilian profit and strategic competitiveness, provided by the skunkworks operations, are important and should be guarded. However, compartmented secrets are necessary for military organizations to support and keep strategic vigilance, and to maintain the support of national security.

It is normal to have some anxiety, some ambiguity, and some level of uncertainty when leaders must operate between the black and white lines of assurance. The greater the assurance required, the more a pragmatic plan for sustaining CCIM. Proactive attempts must first be established by understanding the current state of the organization. Therefore, it is necessary to examine increased assurance from the status quo. Civilian enterprises have luxuries that the military organizations may not have, depending on their adversarial situations. For instance, civilian organizations can more easily review CCIM efforts from less fluid baselines. It is advisable for them to follow CCIM phasing, so that sustainment and continuous improvement can occur, and can be better understood.

Subsequently, at least initially, top down strategies are more efficient during wartime. However, when not in combat, leaders who can adjust and adapt a leadership style that allows more flexibilities and allow others to lead, will get deeper and more sustainable results. As an example, during non-combat operations senior training to study countries and regions can develop "what if" scenarios that can be updated to combine everything discussed in the 3 leg CCIM environments.

Further, those flexibilities that supply actionable results might also have more solution sets and opportunities for the senior manager to consider, when budgets tighten. Combining military and civilian processes may have more benefits, when the goal is to benefit the bottom line, if that bottom line is more constructive and supportive towards sustaining the military member or unit, in the field. Senior managers who understand and support the CCIM process can advance these opportunities. Such occasions might provide better discipline of information security and interface between the military, government civilians, and senior civilian contractor counterparts.

Regardless of the type of organization discussed (civilian, government, military, profit, non-profit) competition exists. Being over-confident in performance or profits, lasts for only a time. It is not forever. According to Pendell (2018), the more success your company or organization have, the more likely you might have those who wish to emulate some, or parts of it, for themselves.

All types of organizations face it. Also, when military organizations, or parts of them, become insolvent or underperforming (Mattis, 2008) they must be amputated while saving the parts of the organization that still performs adequately. Mattis, tasked with oversight of the United States Joint Forces Command, was forced to recommend its closure, at least in part because it did not compete well with its counterparts. Internal cultural conflicts, failed re-organizations, under-estimating competitive organizations, and budgetary constraints played important parts for USJFCOM's failure. [See Chap 2 & Chap 3].

Interruptions in business life-cycles

Business life-cycles are, at least in general, those life cycles that are depicted by the testing, introduction, growth, maturity, decline, and closure of consumer tastes, values, and needs. However, those who subscribe to the simplicity of this general cycle, may fail to realize that different divisions or sections of their organizations may be at different points within that life-cycle.

Why is this important? It is important because business alignments have not occurred. Imagine that production is at a different life cycle than sales, the division may be treated differently by senior managers than if they were on the same life-cycle as most of the organization. Example: PXY industries, makes corrugated cardboard. Production is at capacity and meeting the requirements for the businesses they supply, right now. The sales department is doing a great job selling the corrugated product, and has promised timely delivery to several customers. Those customers have become sold on the product, its quality, and its availability.

The production department has not increased capacity because it was considered in a mature state of their life-cycle. That maturity may be due to outdated equipment, technologies, or space restrictions of the company. Indeed, the senior managers and stakeholders had started looking at plastic containers to replace some of the corrugated product. The sales department had just been expanded and under a dynamic sales team. The newly motivated sales team were rapidly increasing the sales of the corrugated product.

The sales department was in a growth cycle. However, the production department wasn't. The resulting situation caused product delivery promises to become unfulfilled. The mismatch between these two divisions caused an oversight. That oversight created losses for the company in loss of profits, and loss of brand relevance to both their current and future customers.

Also, it is important to realize that different departmental leadership, will have different abilities to change. Some of the more resilient managers have gotten their positions through repetition of those who preceded them, in that same position. Following those steps got them where they were. Some of that is good. However, some of that strict adherence to followership can also adversely affect the alignment, strategic needs, and changes in the division. Further, some of those improvements may be needed for the company to remain profitable.

Again, learning who is capable of change should lead company efforts. Then, it is imperative that senior management explain why the change is needed, so that those managers who must enact those changes see their relevance. Here mentorship matters as attempts ensue to shorten the timeframe so that managers grasp the importance for change involving themselves, their divisions, and the company. The entire organization needs to understand that a steadfast policy, process operations, and aligned procedures can lead to their individual progression and the organization's higher profits.

Figure 4

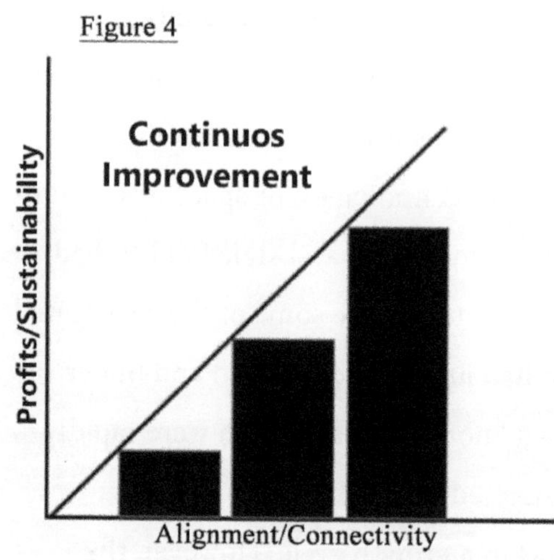

These are some of the reasons why a review of internal processes using the CCIM Three-Leg Stool makes sense. It is easy to miss-step, especially if management leaves divisions within the company out of the planning and input efforts. Trying to assuage people who feel they had no voice, accepted ideas or not, is far more devastating. Also, as described by Farnam Street (2018), your competitor is very likely already planning their strategy and it includes your company or organization, so doing nothing, or doing little in a hap-hazard effort means your company is likely to be already falling behind. Leading from the front can be scary, but senior and middle-management leaders are in positions where they have the opportunity to lead and experience positive outcomes – starting now!

Summary

The speed of business requirements is not slowing, but is becoming increasingly faster. Even if your company or organization is on the right path, they can be by-passed if they stand still long enough. The intent of this book is to help senior managers out-maneuver their competition through learning how to adopt a systems approach to change and continuous improvement management. Second, through the parsing of successful operational segments, this book can help senior managers, middle-managers, and government/military leaders parse that glut of information into an actionable change environment, which can be maintained.

Each independent business discipline source (management, accounting, operational, manufacturing, transportation, etc.) may profess to guide companies to operational nirvana. However, because those independent, and possibly siloed, lenses seldom integrate into a systems approach, they often fail to focus on the overall company or organization's intra-connectiveness. Those lost connections can result in the discoveries of profitable company avenues currently overlooked, which may lead to greater sustainable operations and competitive health.

Also, typical change management efforts most often fail, because the vision to affect continuous improvements is under-developed. Senior management and mid-level managers who utilize Lean, Lean Six Sigma, best practices, balanced scorecards, ORSA, MDMP, PERT, ISO, and various means to affect improvement, often fail to sustain improvements. Typical failures are usually because each tool, when used as a total solution, represents a snap-shot in time and perform analysis that do not align decision making that directly engage their organization's own policies, processes, and procedural standing operations. Snap-shot analysis is just that, but without strategic decisional alignments utilizing the CCIM Three-leg Stool senior managers and their executive management teams often fail to affect their cultures, which can enable change and maintain improvement. Further, without the combination of a systems approach to change management and continuous improvement efforts, the sustainment to thwart competitors and build for your company's or organization's future is risky.

Executive contingency planning, involving environments outside the organization's control, should always be a consideration. That is why each business should have business plans. The what if plans allow organizations to adjust from a base of theorized changes when emotions and resources are not what they need to be to make sound decisions, otherwise. Without a base during such situations, it is easy to be overwhelmed when you have so many relying on decisions during crises.

The CCIM Three-Leg Stool, involves alignments of all business aspects so they not only make sense, but can also provide steps so that production and organizational co-dependent profitability can be enhanced. Pragmatic systems integrations and realistic updates, can support connective business change and improvements. Practicing these resource alignment steps may allow small businesses, U.S. companies, and organizations to once again take the lead in their respective specialties.

Systemic and pragmatic change steps that are achievable for those managers and employees while focusing on the solutions that are best for the entire organization's future successes, will be the right answer. Finding out the proper mix in your organization to support that mission is crucial, to both operational and competitive sustainability. Believing otherwise, leads to the risk of your own company's obsolescence.

References

Accurate Personnel Services (2019). Retraining vs. firing an employee: what should you do? Retrieved from https://www.accurateusa.com/

Advicenow (2019). How do you disseminate your information? Retrieved from https://www.advicenow.org.uk/

Alfredo, D. (2017). The relationship between government & business. *Classroom*. Retrieved from https://classroom.synonym.com/the-relationship-between-government-business-12079488.html

Alton, L. (2017). Phone calls, texts or email? here's how millennials prefer to communicate. *Forbes*, May, 2017. Retrieved from https://www.forbes.com/#6aea7db92254

America Counts Staff (2019). 2020 census will help policymakers prepare for the incoming wave of aging boomers. *U.S. Census Bureau*. Retrieved from https://www.census.gov/library/stories/2019/12/by-2030-all-baby-boomers-will-be-age-65-or-older.html

Arnold, F. (2012). What makes great leaders great. New York: McGraw Hill.

Asplund, J., Leibbrandt, M. & Robison, J. (2020). How strengths, wellbeing and engagement reduce burnout. *Gallup-Cliftonstrengths*. Retrieved from https://www.gallup.com/cliftonstrengths/en/312467/strengths-wellbeing-engagement-reduce-burnout.aspx

Bartels, A. (2017). Global tech market will grow by 4% in 2018, reaching $3 trillion. *Forbes.* Retrieved from https://www.forbes.com/#7b4d0f072254

Benjamin, T. (n.d.). Generational Characteristics of the Workplace. *Small Business - Chron.com*. Retrieved from https://www.chron.com/

Ben-Porat, A. (1981). Event and agent: Toward a structural theory of job satisfaction. *Personnel Psychology, 34*(3), 523-534. Retrieved from doi.org/10.1111/j.1744-6570. 1981.tb00493.x

Bergen, M. & Peteraf, M. (2002). Competitor identification and competitor analysis: A broad-based managerial approach. *Managerial and Decision Economics-Manage, Decisions, Economics*, 157-169. doi:10.1002/mde.1059

Bray, D. (2017). Three meaningful strategies for managing rapid change. *MITSloan Management Review*. Retrieved from https://sloanreview.mit.edu/

Brest, P. (2010). The power of theories of change. Stanford University Graduate School of Business. *Stanford Social Innovation Review*,8(2), 46-51. Retrieved from http://web. ebscohost.com. ezp. waldenulibrary.org/ehost/detail? sid=6ad88b03-8ff2-4e61-af44-1485a4e70bec%40sessionmgr113&vid=1&hid =110&bdata =JnNpd GU9ZW hvc3 QtbGl2ZSZzY29wZT1zaXRl#db =sih&AN=54023205

Careerbuilder (Aug 03, 2018). CareerBuilder's midyear job forecast shows tough hiring environment for employers is paying off for job seekers. Retrieved from https://www.prnewswire.com/news-releases/careerbuilders-midyear-job-forecast-shows-tough-hiring-environment-for-employers-is-paying-off-for-job-seekers-300691139.html

Catalyst (2019, Nov 07). Generations-demographic trends in population and workforce: quick take. Retrieved from https://www.catalyst.org/research/generations-demographic-trends-in-population-and-workforce/

Colrus, B. (2019). 9 ways to improve communication across your organization. *Text Request.* Retrieved from https://www.textrequest.com/

Corr, S. (2018). The effects of the political environment on business organizations. *Bizfluent.* Retrieved from https://bizfluent.com/info-8377458-effects-political-environment-business-organizations.html

Craig, W. (2018). The nature of leadership in a flat organization. *Small Business-Forbes.* Retrieved from https://www.forbes.com/#4769b7212254

Creswell, J. (2014). *Research design.* Los Angeles, CA: Sage.

Danziger, P. (2019). Retail downsizing will accelerate, with ubs predicting 75,000 stores will be forced to close by 2026. *Forbes.* Retrieved from https://www.forbes.com/ #575377852254

Davidson, K., & Restuccia, A. (2019). Trump to sign executive order requiring agencies to offset administrative spending costs. *The Wall Street Journal.* Retrieved from https://www.wsj.com/

DefendX Software (2018). The data security 8-step checklist (2018) [Whitepaper]. Retrieved from https://info.defendx.com/data-security-8-step-checklist-0?gclid=CjwKCAiArK_f BRABEiwA0gOOc2kLIO54ptZNt5rRlJTKw ZGIShPGqx GtjDighPN2AdoBJwI3QZ 7PaRoClcAQAvD_BwE

DeLong, David (2017). Help Your Multigenerational Workforce Thrive. *Smart Workforce Strategies.* Retrieved from https://www.smartworkforcestrategies.com/speaking-consulting-services/multigenerational-workforce-issues/

Diamond, J. (2019). How flat organizations become toxic. *The Startup.* Retrieved from https://medium.com/swlh/how-flat-organizations-become-toxic-efb6c0f59a3a

Dvorak, N. & Nelson, B. (2016). Few employees believe in their company's values. Gallup-Business Journal. Retrieved from https://news.gallup.com

Early, R. (2019). Six tips on cross-cultural communication. *theSource.* Retrieved from https://source.wustl.edu/

Engle, P. (2013). Silos are meant to be broken. *Industrial Engineer, 45*(7), 18. Retrieved from http://www.iienet2.org/IEMagazine/Issue.aspx?IssueMonth=07&IssueYear =2013

Englund,W. (2020). Millions of baby boomers are getting caught in the country's broken retirement system. *Washington Post-Business.* Retrieved from https://www.washington post.com/

Ernst & Young LLP (2013). Younger managers rise in the ranks: survey quantifies management shift and reveals challenges, preferred workplace perks, and perceived generational strengths and weaknesses. *Ciston.* New York: Ernst & Young LLP, 3 September 2013. Retrieved from https://www.prnewswire.com/

Ewenstein, B., Smith, W., & Sologa., A. (2015). Changing change management. McKinsey & Company. Retrieved from https://www.mckinsey.com/

Farnam Street (2018). Strategy vs. tactics: what's the difference and why does it matter? *Farnam Street.* Retrieved from https://fs.blog/

Farrier, T. (2017). *Overcoming the adverse impact of internal subculture communications within organizations.* (Doctoral Dissertation, Walden University). Retrieved from https:// scholarworks.waldenu.edu/cgi/viewcontent.cgi?article=4450&context=dissertations

Faught, S. (2016). When does communication turn into miscommunication? A case study. *International Journal of the Academic Business World, 10*(2), 27-31.

Fleming, J. and Witters, D. (2012). Your employees don't "get" your brand. *Gallup -Business Journal.* Retrieved from https://www.gallup.com/home.aspx

Forbes Technology Council (2018). 12 suggestions to upgrade your business's tech in 2018. Retrieved from https://www.forbes.com/#2a1579b42254

Freeland, G. (2018). Oh no, not another reorganization! do we really need one? *Forbes.* Retrieved from https://www.forbes.com/#174f9d0d2254

Fry, R. (2017). Millennials are the largest generation in the u.s. labor force. *Pew Research.* Retrieved from http://www.pewresearch.org/fact-tank/2018/04/11/millennials-largest-generation-us-labor-force/

Fuhl, J. (2019). 5 ways to manage a multi-generational workforce. *Sage.* Retrieved from https://www.sagepeople.com/about-us/news-hub/five-ways-manage-multi-generational-workforce/

Gandhi, V. (2018). Do Your Employees Have Buyer's Remorse? *Gallup-Workforce.* Retrieved from https://www.gallup.com/workplace/243650/employees-buyer-remorse.aspx? g_source=link_NEWSV9&g_medium=TOPIC&g_campaign=item_

&g_content=Do%2520Your%2520Employees%2520Have%2520 Buyer%27s%2520Remorse%3f

Ghosh, B., Burden, A., & Wilson, J. (2019). Full value - full stop: future systems can help you scale innovation and achieve full value. Retrieved from https://www.accenture.com/us-en

Glassdoor Team (2016). Employee benefits: What each generation wants. *Glassdoor For Employers.* Retrieved from https://www.glassdoor.com

Gownder, J.P., Le Clair, C., Martorelli, B., et al. (2019). Predictions 2019: automation. *Forrester.* Retrieved from https://www.forrester.com

Gravells, J. (2006). The myth of change management: A reflection on personal change and its lessons for leadership development. *Human Resource Development International,* 2, 283-289. doi:10.1080/13678860600616222

Blakely-Gray, R. (2019, April 30). Are you thinking about business reorganization? [*Patriot*]. Retrieved from https://www.patriotsoftware.com/blog/accounting/business-reorganization-types/

Gunn, R., & Gullickson, B. (2006). Learning your suppleness quotient. *Strategic Finance*, 11-12. Retrieved from https://sfmagazine.com

Hamel, G. & Prahalad, C.K. (1996). Competing for the Future. Boston, MA, Harvard Business School Press.

Harter, J., & Agrawal, S. (2014). Many Baby Boomers Reluctant to Retire: Engaged, financially struggling boomers more likely to work longer -Gallup-Economy. Retrieved from https://news.gallup.com/poll/166952/baby-boomers-reluctant-retire.aspx

Harter, J., Agrawal, S., and Sorenson, S. (2014). Jobs outlook grim in countries with more disengaged workers - employee engagement. *Gallup*. Retrieved from https://news.gallup.com/poll/179096/jobs-outlook-grim-countries-disengaged-workers.aspx

Harter, J. (2019). Why some leaders have their employees' trust, and some don't. *Gallup*. Retrieved from https://www.gallup.com/workplace/258197/why-leaders-employees-trust-don.aspx

Heibutzki, Ralph. (2018). Why Is Effective Communication Important in Management? *Work - Chron.com*. Retrieved from http://work.chron.com/effective-communication-important-management-27001.html

Heidari-Robinson, S. & Heywood, S. (2016). Reorg: How to get it right. Boston, Massachusetts. Harvard Business Review Press.

Hopp, A. (2016). Human capital – creating leadership and engagement through better communications. *Strategic HR Review, 15*(1), 1. doi:10.1108/SHR-11-2015-0093

Info Entrepreneurs (2009). Understand your competitors. *Canada Business Network*. Retrieved from https://www.infoentrepreneurs.org/en/

Jensen, C. (2017). My organization just reached 50 employees—what do i need to do? *Employers Council*. Retrieved from https://blog.employerscouncil.org/2017/03/30/my-organization-just-reached-50-employees-what-do-i-need-to-do/

Kaplan, R. & Norton, D. (2006). Alignment, p. 34. United States: Harvard Business School.

Kaplan, R. & Norton, D. (2006). Alignment, p. 96-97. United States: Harvard Business School.

Kaplan, R. & Norton, D. (2006). Alignment, p. 245. United States: Harvard Business School.

Kasasa, (2020, July 22). Boomers, Gen X, Gen Y, and Gen Z Explained. Retrieved from https://www.kasasa.com/articles/generations/gen-x-gen-y-gen-z

kmj23, (2016). Why does the government intervene in business activities? *eNotes*, Retrieved from https://www.enotes.com/homework-help/reasons-government-intervention-business-350017

Kearns, M. (2012). Experiments in Social Computation. *Communications of the ACM*, Vol. 55(10), 56-67. doi:10.1145/2347736.2347753

Kenton, W. (2019). Relationship management. *Investopedia*. Retrieved from https://www. investopedia.com/terms/r/relationship-management.asp

Korman, G. & Klapper, M. (1978). Game theory's wartime connections and the study of industrial conflict. *Industrial and Labor Relations Review*. Retrieved from doi:10. 2307/2522416

Kotter, J. (1996). *Leading Change*. Harvard Business Review Press. Boston, Massachusetts

Kramer, L. (2019). Companies employ to increase market share? *Investopedia*. Retrieved from https://www.investopedia.com/ask/answers/031815/what-strategies-do-companies-employ-increase-market-share.asp

La Loggia, B. (2018). 5 Secrets to Managing a Multi-Generational Workforce. *American Express Open Forum*. Retrieved from https://www.americanexpress.com/us/small-business/openforum/articles/5-secrets-managing-multi-generational-workforce/

Le Clair, C. (2019). How automation is impacting enterprises in 2019. Forrester. Retrieved from https://go.forrester.com/

Lin, T. (2019). Facilitating multi-generational talent collaboration in a context-critical world through design capabilities. *Management Studies, 7*(6), 523-532. doi: 10.17265/2328-2185/2019.06.002

Levine, N. (2017). The nature of the glut: Information overload in postwar America. *History of the Human Sciences, 30*(1), 32–49. doi:10.1177/0952695116686016

Madsen, T. (2019). The 5 most important soft skills of the future. *e-Learning Industry.* Retrieved from https://elearningindustry.com/

Mattis, J. (2008). USJFCOM commander's guidance for effects-based operations. *Parameters.* Retrieved from http://ssi.armywarcollege.edu/pubs/parameters/Articles/08autumn/

mattis.pdf

McDermott, K., Spence-Lashinger, H.K., and Shamian, J. (1996). Work empowerment and organizational commitment. *Nursing Management, 27*(5), *44-47.* doi: 10.1097/00006247-199605000-00010

McKim, C. (2017). The value of mixed methods research: A mixed methods study. *Journal of Mixed Methods Research-Sage, 11*(2), 202-226. doi: 10.1177/1558689815607096

Neals, S. & Wellins, R., (2018). Generation x-not millennials-is changing the nature of work. *Make It.* Retrieved from https://www.cnbc.com/2018/04/11/generation-x--not-millennials--is-changing-the-nature-of-work.html

Opinion Front (2019). Major social issues that are prevalent in the united states. *Opinion Front.* Retrieved from https://opinionfront.com/social-issues-in-united-states

Patrick, C., & Sundaram, D. (2018). The Real Value of Getting an Exit Interview Right. *Gallup-Business Journal-Workplace.* Retrieved from https://www.gallup.com/workplace /236051/real-value-getting-exit-interview-right.aspx?g_source=link_NEWSV9&g_medium=&g_campaign=item_&g_content=The%2520Real%2520Value%2520of%2520Getting%2520an%2520Exit%2520Interview%2520RightGen

Pacheco, G., & Webber, D. (2016). Job satisfaction: how crucial is participative decision making? *Personnel Review, 45*(1), 183–200. doi:10.1108/PR-04-2014-0088

Pendell, R. (2018). 6 scary numbers for your organization's c-suite. *Gallup-Workplace.* Retrieved at https://www.gallup.com/topic/all_gallup_headlines.aspx

Pew Research Center (2014). The generations defined. *Pew Research.* Retrieved from http://www. pewsocialtrends.org/2014/03/07/millennials-in-adulthood/sdt-next-america-03-07-2014-0-06/

Purcell, P. (2000). Older workers: employment and retirement trends. Monthly Labor Review- October 2000. Retrieved from https://www.bls.gov/opub/mlr/2000/10/art3full.pdf

Quick take: Generations—demographic trends in population and workforce (2018). *Catalyst.* Retrieved from https://www.catalyst.org/research/generations-demographic-trends-in-population-and-workforce/

Rampton, J. (2017). Different motivations for different generations of workers: Boomers, gen X, millennials, and gen Z, *Inc.* Retrieved from https://www.inc.com/john-rampton/different-motivations-for-different-generations-of-workers-boomers-gen-x-millennials-gen-z.html

Ratanjee, V. (2018). Focus on the Positive: A new approach to change management. *Gallup-Workplace*. Retrieved from https://www.gallup.com/workplace/238166/focus-positive-new-approach-change-management.aspx?g_source=link_NEWSV9&g_medium= TOPIC&g_campaign=item_&g_content=Focus%2520on%2520the%2520Positive%3a%2520A%2520New%2520Approach%2520to%2520Change%2520Management

Ray, L. (2017). Social & cultural risks in business. *Bizfluent*. Retrieved from https://bizfluent.com/info-7993593-social-cultural-risks-business.html

Richardson, T. (2007). Why focusing on processes is the holy grail of business management. *Management Services, 51*(3). Retrieved from https://www.questia.com/

Ridge, G., (2018) The Learning Moment. *The Learning Moment*. Retrieved from https://thelearningmoment.net/

Rigoni, B., Asplund, J., and Sorenson, S. (2014). Baby Boomers Not Maximizing Their Strengths: Strengths differ slightly by generation. *Gallup-Well Being*. Retrieved from https://news.gallup.com/poll/166997/baby-boomers-not-maximizing-strengths.aspx

Robinson, S., and Heywood, S. (2016). Getting reorgs right. *Harvard Business Review, 11*(6), 84-89. Retrieved from https://hbr.org/2016/11/getting-reorgs-right

Saberton, M. (2018, September 1). Avoiding operational silos. [Huddle] Retrieved from https://www.huddle.com /blog/ breaking-operational-silos

Sammer, J. (2018). Welcome, generation z: Here's your benefits package. *SHRM*. Retrieved from https://www.shrm.org/ ResourcesAndTools/hr-topics/benefits/Pages/generation-z-benefits-package.aspx

Samuelson, K. (2018). 'I Personally Apologize.' Starbucks CEO Kevin Johnson Speaks Out After Black Men Arrested in Philadelphia Store. Time. Retrieved from https://time.com/5241 426/ starbucks-ceo-apology-philadelphia/

Sanow, A. (2013). 25 things customers love-create a customer service mindset. *Leaders Beacon*. Retrieved from https://www. leadersbeacon.com/category/leadership/customer-service/

Santos, M.V. & Garcia, M.T. (2006). Organizational change: The role of managers' mental models. *Journal of Change Management*, 5(4), 315-320. Retrieved from https://www.tandfonline.com. doi:10.1080/14697010600963084

Schawbel, D. (2017, February 3). 53 of the most interesting facts about baby boomers. [*Dan Schawbel]*. Retrieved from https:// danschawbel. com/blog/53-of-the-most-interesting-facts-about-baby-boomers/

Schein, E. (2019). A new era for culture, change, and leadership with Dr. Edgar Schein/ Interviewer: Peter Schein (June 25). MIT Management Review. Retrieved from https://sloanreview.mit.edu/ article/a-new-era-for-culture-change-and-leadership/?use_ credit =f9429cbcd6a95dba7e2840a8afc248fa&fbclid=IwAR3ie0aw ByrtPw78unvtJyKyqXzgLjfx32Ylt5vYIK37X2w8uWvaoNieIak

Senge, P. (2006). The fifth discipline: The art and practice of the learning organization. Currency Publishing.

Silic, M., & Back, A. (2016). Factors driving unified communications and collaboration adoption and use in organizations. *Measuring Business Excellence, 20*(1), 1–25. doi:10.1108/MBE-05-2015-0026

Singh, K. (2020). Is your business continuity plan missing 2 key pieces? *Workplace-Gallup*. Retrieved from https://www.gallup.com/workplace/312800/business-continuity-plan-missing-key-pieces.aspx

Sorenson, S., Garman, K. (2013). There's a Generation Gap in Your Workplace. Gallup-*Business Journal,* August 6. Retrieved from https://www.gallup.com/home.aspx

Span, S. (2019). Lack of trust in leadership is the biggest issue impacting performance – how do you fix the problem? *Tolero Solutions*. Retrieved from https://tolerosolutions.com/ employees-lack-trust-in-leadership-biggest-issue-impacting-performance/

Statista (2020). Forecast of the U.S. Gross Domestic Product (GDP) for fiscal years 2019 to 2030 (in billions of U.S. dollars). Retrieved from https://www.statista.com/

Tabaka, M. (2019). Gen-z will make up 24 percent of the global workforce in 2020. here's what employers need to know. *Inc.*, Retrieved from https://www.inc.com/

Tams, C. (2018). Why we need to rethink organizational change management. *Forbes Now*. Retrieved from https://www.forbes.com/#40dd2792254c

Tatum, S. (2019). Proposed trump administration policy pushes for transparency in health care costs. Retrieved from https://abcnews.go.com/Politics/proposed-trump-administration-policy-pushes-transparency-health-care/story?id=67043874

Ten Six (2017). How to avoid (bad) surprises on projects. Retrieved from https://tensix.com/

The Community Toolbox (2015). Chapter 8, Section 5, Developing an action plan. Work Group for Community Health and Development at the University of Kansas. Retrieved from http://ctb.ku.edu/en

Todnem By, R., Kuipers, B., and Procter, S. (2018). Understanding teams in order to understand organizational change: The otic model of organizational change. *Journal of Change Management, 18*(1), 1-9, doi:10.1080/14697017.2018.1433742

Tope, O. (2017). Task-oriented versus relationship-oriented leadership styles: Perceptions of the Nigerian work environment. *International Journal of Economics- Commerce and Management,* 5(11), 414-435: United Kingdom. Retrieved from http://ijecm.co.uk/

Toossi, M. (2013). Labor force projections to 2022: the labor force participation rate continues to fall. *Monthly Labor Review,* U.S. Bureau of Labor Statistics. doi.org/10.21916/mlr. 2013.40

Toossi, M. (2015) "Labor force projections to 2024: the labor force is growing, but slowly," *Monthly Labor Review,* U.S. Bureau of Labor Statistics. doi.10.21916/mlr.2015.48

Toossi, M. (2016). A look at the future of the U.S. labor force to 2060. *U.S. Department of Labor Statistics,* September, 1-12. Retrieved from https://www.bls.gov/spotlight/2016/a-look-at-the-future-of-the-us-labor-force-to-2060/pdf/a-look-at-the-future-of-the-us-labor-force-to-2060.pdf

Turnage, A. K., & Goodboy, A. K. (2016). E-mail and face-to-face organizational dissent as a function of leader-member exchange status. *International Journal of Business Communication, 53*(3), 271-285. doi:10.1177/2329488414525456

Ukman, J. (2011, August 4). U.S. joint forces command officially dissolved. *The Washington Post.* Retrieved from https://www.washingtonpost.com/blogs/checkpoint-washington/ post/us-joint-forces-command-formally-dissolved/2011/08/04/gIQAQbzBuI _ blog.html

University of East Anglia. (2016, February 1). Restructuring affects staff well-being regardless of job cuts. *ScienceDaily.* Retrieved from https://www.sciencedaily.com/releases/2016/02/160201220120.htm

U.S. Census Bureau (2018, March 13). Older people projected to outnumber children for first time in u.s. history. Retrieved from https://www.census.gov/newsroom/press-releases/2018/cb18-41-population-projections.html

U.S. Department of Labor-Bureau of Labor Statistics (2017, October 24). Economic news release-employment projections: 2016-26 summary. *U.S. Department of Labor-Bureau of Labor Statistics.* Retrieved from https://www.bls.gov/news.release/archives/ecopro _10242017.pdf

U.S. Department of Labor-Bureau of Labor Statistics (2018). Black workers' share of the total labor force, 1972-2016, and projected to 2026. *U.S. Department of Labor-Bureau of Labor Statistics.* Retrieved from https://www.bls.gov/spotlight/2018/blacks-in-the-labor-force/home.htm

U.S. Department of Labor-Bureau of Labor Statistics (2018). Employee tenure summary. *U.S. Department of Labor-Bureau of Labor Statistics.* Retrieved from https://www.bls.gov/news.release/tenure.nr0.htm

U.S. Bureau of Labor Statistics (2018). Household data annual averages - employment status of the civilian noninstitutional population by age, sex, and race. Retrieved from https://www.bls.gov/home.htm

U.S. Department of Labor-Bureau of Labor Statistics (2019). Economic news release- employment projections: 2018-2028 Summary. Retrieved from https://www.bls.gov/ news.release/ecopro.nr0.htm

Why does the government intervene in business activities? *eNotes Editorial*, 23 July 2012, https://www.enotes.com/homework-help/reasons-government-intervention-business-350017. Accessed 29 Jan. 2020.

Wisdom, J. (2019, August 2). How to thrive in a multi-generational workplace. *Training Industry.* Retrieved from https://trainingindustry.com/

Wulf, J. (2012). The flattened firm - not as advertised. *Harvard Business School.* Retrieved from https://hbswk.hbs.edu/item/the-flattened-firmnot-as-advertised

Yemm, G. (2007). Change management - encouraging successful change. *Management Services, 51*(1), 40. Retrieved from https://www.expertbase.org/a258-encouraging-successful-change

Yohn, D. (2019). Marketing matters now more than ever. *Forbes.* Retrieved from https:// www.forbes.com/

Zerfass, A., Vercic, D. & Wiesenberg, M. (2016). Managing CEO communication and positioning: A cross-national study among corporate communication leaders. *Journal of Communication Management, 20*(1), 37–55. doi:10.1108/JCOM-11-2014-0066

About the Author

Terrence L. Farrier, Ph.D., MSS, MBA

As a business consultant since 1992, Dr. Farrier has worked with small and medium sized companies to better integrate and help them increase their profits. He explains that all businesses are different even if they appear the same. Their customer base, location, environments, competition and so on affect the overall business in ways that are not immediately noticeable.

Dr. Farrier earned his Doctor of Philosophy in Applied Management Decision Sciences from Walden University in 2017 while acting as an adviser and consultant to both civilian and military groups. He earned his Master's in Strategic Studies from the U.S. Army War College in 2005, and Master's in Business Administration from Regis University in 2001. He also earned a BS/BA in Human Resources and Marketing Management from the U of A, Fayetteville, AR in 1989. He had a long military career and acted in support of think tanks for the Army Reserve. Some of his overseas positions included duties as the Transition Officer for Logistics Battalions and Brigades in Europe in 2004. As a LTC (ret) Army Reserve Officer, his military career also encompassed duties as part of the Command Advisor Group for U.S. Joint Forces Command as the Personnel Support and Enterprise Transition Officer from 2005 to 2007. His military and civilian capacities while overseas were as Commander for a Contracts Supervision Unit, to support the Eighth U.S. Army in

Korea in logistics capacities, and II MEF (Fwd) Regional Command's (RC) C-3 Operations as the Tactical IT Systems Administrator. He sees his primary skill as an organizer, trainer, facilitator, and integrator of systems management that promotes both skill and pride for those in management roles. He believes that you must learn to love people, even if you have to learn to love some at a distance.

Lightning Source UK Ltd.
Milton Keynes UK
UKHW012012070621
385112UK00001B/29

9 781665 515351